The Simple
Abundance
Companion

Also by Sarah Ban Breathnach

Sarah Ban Breathnach

The Simple Abundance Companion

Following Your Authentic Path
to Something More

WARNER BOOKS

A Time Warner Company

Grateful acknowledgment is given for permission to reprint "Phenomenal Woman" from *And I Still Rise* by Maya Angelou. Copyright © 1978 by Maya Angelou. Reprinted by permission of Random House, Inc.

THE ILLUSTRATED DISCOVERY JOURNAL™ and AUTHENTIC SELF™ are trademarks of Simple Abundance, Inc. SIMPLE ABUNDANCE® is a registered trademark of Sarah Ban Breathnach. The moral rights of the author have been asserted.

Something More™ is a trademark of Simple Abundance®, Inc.

Portions of this book were taught in workshop settings at the Chautauqua Institution, Chautauqua, New York, in 1993, 1994, 1995, 1996; at the Disney Institute, Orlando, Florida, in 1996; and at the Omega Institute, Rhinebeck, New York, in 1997.

The following portions of this book first appeared as written material during 1998–1999 in *Good Housekeeping* magazine: pages 7–9, 91–94, 175–181, 189.

Warner Books, Inc., 1271 Avenue of the Americas, New York, NY 10020
Visit our Web site at www.twbookmark.com

 A Time Warner Company

Printed in the United States of America
First Printing: April 2000

10 9 8 7 6 5 4

Library of Congress Cataloging-in-Publication Data
Ban Breathnach, Sarah.
    The simple abundance companion : following your authentic path to something more / Sarah Ban Breathnach.
        p.   cm.
    ISBN 0-446-67333-1
    1. Women—Religious life.   2. Meditations.   I. Ban Breathnach, Sarah. Simple abundance.   II. Title.
    BL625.7 .B352   2000
    158.1'2—dc21   99-049015

Cover design by Diane Luger
Cover illustration by Margaret Chodos-Irvine
Book design and text composition by Ralph Fowler
Interior illustrations by Jackie Aher

I suppose there is one friend in the life of each of us who seems not a

separate person, however dear and beloved, but an expansion,

an interpretation, of one's self, the very meaning of one's soul.

EDITH WHARTON

For You

With love and gratitude. My journey would

not have been the same without your

dear and beloved eyes.

Contents

Contents

Introduction

*To teach one's self is to be
forced to learn twice.*

ELLEN GLASGOW,
THE WOMAN WITHIN (1954)

In the beginning, *Simple Abundance* was the workshop not the word. For several years before my book was published in 1995, I taught *Simple Abundance* to women very much like myself and you. Women who hurdle through life as if it were an out-of-body experience. Women who love everyone else on the planet too much and themselves too little. Because my memories of those early mysterious encounters (for I was feeling and writing my way into the future, as well as guiding others) were so pleasurable, so was creating this book.

A workshop can be a wondrous experience or a tedious disappointment (there doesn't seem to be any in-between), depending, of course, on the attitude and attentiveness that both lecturer and participant bring to it. I've led seminars and I've been the hostess of some swell parties. Like any social gathering or relationship (and workshops are both), the most successful ones seem fated, even magical. Over the space of a few hours or days, a great exchange between complete strangers takes place as extravagant, reciprocal gifts of time, creative energy and emotion are generously bestowed and gratefully received.

Dr. Ira Progoff, the creator of "The Intensive Journal" workshop, the seminal model for group self-help programs since the early seventies, describes the ideal workshop as a place for solitary work that cannot be done alone. "The presence of others, each engaged in reaching into the past and potentials of his own life, seems to have the effect of assisting the solitary work of everyone." In this ideal workshop, "we are shielded from the outer pressures of our life. In a sense we are withdrawing from those pressures, but not in order to escape from them." Rather, we withdraw so that we might fully engage our hearts and minds to consider "the truly fundamental questions and issues of our lives."

That is what you and I will be doing together on these pages. Withdrawing to consider.

Even when an author leads a workshop based on her own book, the material cannot be presented in the same way. If it is, it will seem skimpy—a frisée salad of insights—when compared to the meat and potatoes of observations bound together between two covers. This is why I've always tried to design my Simple Abundance and Something More workshops to stand alone. Since there was no book in the beginning, this was accomplished with a lot of handouts! But even after there were books, I wanted each workshop to be its own authentic experience. This desire continues with *The Simple Abundance Companion: Following Your Authentic Path to Something More*. This time I've culled a year's worth of lessons for us to ponder, mull over, meditate upon, work through, and hopefully process so they will sink in and we can move on to enjoy the life that's waiting for us.

Why these particular soul assignments? Because tolerating well is not living well, and unfortunately the spiritual curriculum of the Cosmos is not optional. Some of these life lessons are ones I've embraced, embodied, and swear by. I consider them secrets meant to be shared; they've transformed my life in wondrous ways, which is why I want to help you master them. Then there are those lessons that try my soul during the day and haunt me during dark nights. Don't let lipstick, high heels, and being on the best-seller list fool you. Learning to let go, surrendering expectations, and getting out of my own way are challenges I keep having to work through, over and over. And over again. Maybe this year with you is the last time I'll have to do them.

Always remember, it's one thing for us to understand something intellectually, it's quite another for spiritual truth to register emotionally. And until it does, it's repeat and return. Return and repeat. Some of the lessons I've chosen were born on the pages of *Simple Abundance* and *Something More,* and some of them occurred during my own continuing journey. But whether you've read these books or not, hopefully the exercises and ideas between the covers of the book that you hold in your hands now can serve as a catalyst for your own explorations.

So please consider this workbook a personal tutorial. Just you and me. Maybe add a few of your closest pals. But please, think girls' night out instead of study group as we sift and sort. I've *finally* learned to choose fun over earnestness any day of the week, and I'm not going back.

As for our approach, the Russian writer Nina Berberova believed that there were two laws to be obeyed when writing down your life for soulful reflection: "The first, reveal yourself completely. The second, conceal your life for yourself alone." That is why I want you to be very careful with whom you share this workbook and its main insight tools—your Gratitude Journal and your Illustrated Discovery Journal. I share mine *only* with my Authentic Self and I urge you to create the same boundaries. By all means, take advantage of the energy and creativity generated through working in a group setting if you wish, but do so privately.

You're about to discover what the writer Ellen Glasgow meant when she observed in *The Woman Within* that those of us who teach ourselves get to learn things twice. At the very least. But before any *how-to* spiritual or lifestyle guide can shift the trajectory of our thinking, we have to understand the *why-to*. Personally I don't think soul growth occurs because the student is ready and a spiritual teacher appears. I believe it's much more the case that when the soul is genuinely ready to release pain, *the lesson kicks in.*

As in, "By Jove, I think she's got it." That is the prayer of this workbook, to help us "get it," whatever the particular *it* might be in your life right now. Mine changes frequently, I suspect yours does too, which is why we'll withdraw to consider one chapter a month.

Now to get to work.

As we begin, a few thoughts on approach. Despite its description as a "workbook," *The Simple Abundance Companion* invites you to play yourself into well-being, rather than "work" yourself into a frenzy, however well-intentioned. In order to do that we're going to have to abandon our familiar patterns. Authenticity is no right-brain "thinking" thing. She's a left-brain babe who feels her way through life. If you have to think of anything, think of Benny Goodman's swing romp "In the Mood," because "moodling" is the easiest way to spiritually induce authentic moments of emotional clarity.

What is moodling? The incomparable writer Brenda Ueland, who coined the word, explains that it's "long, inefficient, happy idling, dawdling and puttering" that induces revealing and rewarding reveries.

So, while there is space at the end of these chapters to address specific questions, I want you to consider the rather large moodling margins throughout this workbook as the place for random thoughts, doodles, ah-*ha*'s and *isn't that interesting* hmm's waiting to flirt with you.

Creating your own soulful atmosphere is important. The reassuring rhythm of a private interlude carved out of a busy week, set aside, much anticipated, and *inviolate,* is crucial, as is a nook of your own—a quiet spot to beat a retreat for reading, writing, and reflecting. Listening to some beautiful instrumental music and indulging in favorite refreshments enhances the learning curve, at least for me.

Throughout these pages you're going to find a variety of personal prompts—exercises, questions, meditations, affirmations, and new approaches to solving old problems—meant to elicit a participatory response from you. Being authentic is being unique, so some techniques might work better for you than others. All I ask is that you be open, try them, and see what happens. (What the heck? It can't hurt.) You'll also find suggestions for three of my favorite forms of introspection—*cinematherapy, audiotherapy,* and *bibliotherapy.* Included are some movies, music, and reading that are dearly beloved by me but may be new to you. These suggestions are how I nourish my soul and I recommend them to you with pleasure.

In addition, because this is a workbook for you, by you, and about you, I have included space for you to follow my lead in creating your own meditations—an extremely powerful insight tool that I first discovered while writing *Simple Abundance.* When I began that project, one of the ways I readied myself for daily writing was to choose a quote. I had been collecting quotes for years and had boxes of them, so finding a new one each day was easy. Once I would write out the quote longhand, I found that it stirred all sorts of memories in me, and I was able to go directly to the computer and write a piece stemming from the quote. This exercise is wonderful, because it allows you to pull stories out of your own life. You'll be amazed and inspired by the personal relevance of a quote—and exploring these meanings grants enormous insights into your authentic self.

Consider using the quotes I've found for you at the end of each chapter as starting points for writing your own authentic meditations. Start slowly. Search for the Sacred in your ordinary life, and it will be revealed as extraordinary.

In my books I often use the word "Spirit" for God, because I do not want to impose on my readers my own view of Divinity, which is always expanding, thank Heaven. Please be open to the vastness of the Divine. In many spiritual traditions, there isn't even a word for God. The Authentic Self, for me, is your soul made visible.

The search for your Authentic Self is a sacred adventure and a magical undertaking. I am honored that you're inviting me once again to accompany you on your deeply personal journey to Wholeness. I'm grateful, beyond measure, that I'm able to continue mine in your dear company.

Blessings on your courage.

Sarah Ban Breathnach
July 1999

Chapter 1

Welcome to You

*Undoubtedly, we become
what we envisage.*

CLAUDE M. BRISTOL

You are beautiful. Right now. Today. Just as you are, just the way you look as you read those three words: You. Are. Beautiful. Say it slowly aloud, as if the phrase were a foreign language, for it probably is.

You are beautiful. Now say it in the first person singular.

I am beautiful.

Do you know that? If so, remind yourself of this glorious fact every day. If not, it is time to become beautiful in your own eyes. This will require a makeover of sorts, but not the kind you think. Learning to love the way you look has nothing to do with starting a diet or reshaping your eyebrows. Accepting and embracing your authentic beauty means seeing yourself from the inside out. *I love me, I love me not—I love me.*

Beauty may only be skin deep, but there is nothing superficial about the complicated relationship that a woman has with her appearance. How you see yourself and how you think other people see you—your body image—is deeply connected to how you feel about yourself.

Believe in yourself. And believe that there s a loving Source—a Sower of Dreams— just waiting to be asked to help you make your dreams come true.

SIMPLE ABUNDANCE
JANUARY 1

The effects of a negative body image can be devastating. If you don't like the way you look, you probably don't like the woman you are. And those feelings of worthlessness, self-consciousness, and inadequacy will insinuate their way into nearly every area of your life— into your friendships, your career, your romances, and, most importantly, your relationship with yourself.

A positive body image is equally powerful. It is not an instant solution to all of life's problems, but a starting point, a spark that can set off a fabulous chain reaction. Loving how you look when you catch a glimpse of yourself in a mirror or store window paves the path of self-love, and with that acceptance comes self-esteem, confidence, and authentic beauty, a radiance that glows from within. A beauty that is more than skin deep.

Sowing the Seeds of Self

Self-admiration giveth much consolation.

GERTRUDE ATHERTON

Looking in the mirror is a startling subjective experience. When facing her reflection, one woman may say to herself, "I wish my hips were smaller," or "My fat hips make me ugly." Or she could say, "My curves make me sexy." In each example, the hips are the same—it's how a woman feels about them that's different. But where do these feelings come from? Whether or not you realize it, you've spent your entire life developing them, honing them, cloning them. Transforming the messages communicated by society, your family, your friends, your rivals, and your enemies into cellular memory.

"As preschoolers, boys and girls have already learned the lessons about physical appearance that our society teaches," explains psychologist Thomas Cash, author of *What Do You See When You Look in the Mirror?* "They know that lovely Cinderella gets the prince; her ugly and mean stepsisters do not. From childhood on . . . we judge our self-worth by the physical standards we've absorbed." The world's standards—to be extraordinarily thin, conventionally attractive, and forever young—are uncompromising and unrealistic, yet so pervasive in the media that women who do not conform (and who does?) feel flawed, inferior, unsuccessful, unlovable.

Society's ideals are reinforced in children by parents who overemphasize the importance of appearance, consciously or unconsciously. Their messages, be they subtle or painfully obvious, are expressed in dozens of ways: Were you put on a diet as a child or compared unfavorably to a sibling? Or were you praised for your prettiness, made to feel that it was your looks that made you lovable? Did your father disparage your mother for the way she looked? Or did she obsess about her own appearance? Don't discount the influence of friends and classmates: Being teased as a child or ostracized as a teenager can undermine the efforts of the most accepting parents.

Do you have memories of experiences that might have contributed to the way you see yourself today? As an adult, you may be able to "understand" them, to understand that your parents' criticisms did not mean they didn't love you, or that the bullies at school were acting purely out of their own insecurities. But this doesn't make the memories any less hurtful or their hold on you any less powerful. However, facing them, before you face yourself in the mirror, is the crucial first step in reshaping your body image.

A lifetime pattern of self-denigration is not going to disappear overnight. You're going to have to learn how to replace your automatic criticisms with praise. Self-admiration takes many forms. It can and should include the new compliments you pay to yourself everyday. But the most powerful self-compliment of all is honoring the promises you make to your own soul.

Promises, Promises

For where does one run to when [s]he's already in the promised land?

CLAUDE BROWN

During the early seventies I worked in London as a fledgling freelance writer and earned in a flush week about $75. Of necessity, I inhabited a dreary, cheerless cell euphemistically known as a "bed-sitter." It had a hot plate to cook on, a sink, a two-shelf "fridge," and about ten feet of space. The bathroom was down the hall, and every time I wanted to take a hot bath I had to put a shilling into a meter to fire up the furnace for five minutes. But my cell was located off the fashionable Kings Road in Chelsea just around the corner from the studio of an amazing young shoe designer named Manolo Blahnik. Almost every day I would walk by his little mews house, stop and gaze longingly and lovingly at his sophisticated cobbler's confections. But since the price of one pair of his shoes then cost more than a month's rent, my gossamer visions of Old Hollywood glamour precariously perched on three-inch heels were consigned to the vast void of "someday."

I had arrived in England with little more than that glorious unshakable certainty one possesses only between the ages of eighteen and twenty-seven that I could make all my dreams of fame and fortune come true within one year—the window of opportunity ordained by my round-trip excursion fare ticket. When I didn't and only a few days separated me from having to make an excruciating decision—return home or remain abroad—I learned a priceless lesson about the magical, mysterious, and mystical power of promises to reconfigure our future in Divine ways.

In my pocket was the check from my last assignment. If I stayed it would have to take care of the bare necessities—room, board, and ransoming my typewriter from the pawnshop. If truth be told, I was barely surviving; most of the time I was cold and hungry, not to men-

Turn away from the world this year and begin to listen. Listen to the whispers of your heart. Look within. Your silent companion has lit lanterns of love to illuminate the path to Wholeness. At long last, the journey you were destined to take has begun.

SIMPLE ABUNDANCE
JANUARY 5

5

tion psychically and physically exhausted from constant worry about money. (I shudder at the thought of my daughter in a similar situation.) But going home meant not just giving up and giving in, it also meant withering forever under the suffocating smugness of "we told you so"s. Staying meant toughing it out until I got some visible sign that Heaven appreciated my mettle and applauded my moxie.

On the other hand, if I returned home, I could splurge on a pair of Manolo's shoes. But one pair? Just one pair? There were so many beautiful possibilities, I couldn't make up my mind. How could I make such a choice? As absurd as this sounds, the fact that I couldn't choose between the hot pink pumps and the leopard-skin stilettos altered the trajectory of my life. Now I realize that wanting something more out of life than just one pair of shoes was Spirit's way of urging me not to sell myself short, limit my dreams or my flamboyant, passionate, extravagant faith. *Stay, Sarah, and I promise that one day you'll come back here and walk out with as many pairs of Manolo Blahnik shoes as you want.* I stayed.

It took me twenty-five years to be reunited with my sole-mate, but true love withstands the test of time. Those shoes were far more than coveted fashion accessories. They were a symbol of my ultimate commitment to myself. I am blessed to be living most of my dreams but honoring that self-promise was one of the most soul-satisfying things I've ever done. Women are great at delivering on their word when it's someone else counting

on us, but when no one else is looking or listening we re-
nege on ourselves with a ruthlessness that's heartbreak-
ing. At least I know I have.

Promises predict a woman's future better than any
crystal ball ever could. That's because the promises we
make decide how we shall spend, invest, or squander
our Life's currency: time, creative energy, and emotion.
We tend to think through the implications of promises
we've made well after we've already committed to them.
Just ask any woman who has mysteriously found herself
chauffeuring a carload of kids to the mall on a Saturday
afternoon instead of getting a badly needed haircut,
meeting a friend for lunch, or showing up for that yoga
class she's wanted to attend for the last six months.

There are two kinds of promises—Outer and Inner.
Outer promises are those we make to our family, friends,
colleagues, church, the PTA bake sale coordinator. Outer
promises are often unconscious. Think about the absent-
minded nod of assent when you're distracted—when
you're on the phone, perusing papers, or concentrating
on something else. We also tend to promise more than
we can reasonably deliver when we're feeling uncomfortable—when we're coming down with the flu, tired,
worried, depressed, or anxious. Make a rule for yourself:
When your defenses are down, don't promise anything
more than a "maybe."

Outer promises often come disguised as peacemak-
ers because they keep children quiet, get our significant
others to stop nagging, reassure the boss. But promises
offered only to be cooperative or amiable are deceptive

and disruptive. If you dread it, don't agree to do it. If you do end up doing it despite your dread, you'll despise the whole deal and everyone connected to it, including yourself.

Inner promises are those we make to our minds, bodies, and spirits. Join a book club. Start an exercise program. Find an uninterrupted hour a day to call your own. Although self-promises tend to be pleasurable and positive rather than punitive, we rarely keep them. Why? Because without accountability, visibility, pressure, shame, or guilt as our personal prompts we don't think they really matter. We don't believe that our happiness, well-being, or contentment counts for much. If we did we would be considered self-centered. When we break self-promises we are under the illusion that there are no repercussions—after all, we reason, who else knows, cares, or is keeping track of the fact that you can't be counted on?

Our inner promises represent authentic needs and come wrapped up in wishes of "want." Outer promises are gifts we give to others and often are wrapped up in "should." Desire versus Demand. This does not mean that you genuinely don't want to manage the bazaar craft booth, take your elderly aunt to the doctor, or write a glowing recommendation for your friend's daughter. But if you find yourself doing all three in one week it's time you became aware of your personal pattern of promise making.

Can you recall the last five promises you made? (If you can't you've just discovered what I mean by unconscious ones.) Just as there are personal patterns in how we spend money, avoid confrontation, and deal with depression, we've each got a promise pattern based on our need to please. Did you offer or were you asked? If you were asked, did you even register what was requested of you at the time? See if you can recall what prompted you to say yes. We can't change our behavior until we know how we're acting.

A woman I know who is a successful judge recently recalled her graduate school days when she was studying music. She was so poor that she and her roommate would share an opera ticket—one would see the first act, the other the second. She promised herself that someday she'd become so successful she'd sit in the best seat in the house and never even ask what the price was. She confessed proudly that she still feels a small shiver of self-pleasure in continuing to honor her thirty-year-old promise. But not just of her accomplishments in the legal profession. A fourth-row orchestra seat is a powerful reminder that she is the best kind of promise keeper—not only in the eyes of the world but in the eyes of her own soul.

What long-overdue promises to yourself are in your past? This would be a great year to make good on them. A promise is a solemn, sacred prayer and you are a woman worthy of your word.

Like moths drawn to the flame, we flit through our entire lives secretly searching for stolen moments when we can allow ourselves to be swept away by something larger than the life we've settled for.

SOMETHING MORE
"THE HOLY
LONGING"

Catching up with the Dream

Dreams grow holy, put in action.

ADELAIDE ANNE PROCTOR

A dream is a promise you make to Spirit and yourself. Sometimes it takes literally years to keep that promise, whether it's a home, a family, a career, or a lifestyle. Dreams cost sweat, frustration, tears, courage, choices, money, perseverance, and patience. But birthing a dream requires one more thing: Love as the midwife.

There is a dream that only you can bring into the world. Do you know what it is? Or has it been buried under layers of naïveté, good intentions, relinquishment, bitter failures, detours, disappointments, rejections, wrong choices, bad timing, bungled efforts, stupid mistakes, unforeseen circumstances, whims of fate, and missed opportunities? In other words, the rubble of an unconscious life.

But how can you resurrect that dream, when you weren't able to realize it the first time? The difference is that now you know how to make choices, whereas maybe twenty-five years ago you didn't.

So set yourself a realistic deadline in which to bring your dream into reality. If you give yourself a deadline that is feasible—say, four years from now, not four months—by next year you will have taken the first concrete steps toward realizing it. It might be breaking

Sometimes when we awaken from the bad dream of disowning ourselves, we think that the sojourn to self-discovery is a new one. But it is an ancient quest.

SOMETHING MORE
"THE BOOK OF LOVE"

10

ground for a new house. It might be renting a storefront. It might be finishing the first draft of a book. I don't know what it is for you but you do. And if you've not discovered it yet, continue doing this process and you should discover it by the end of the year.

Dreams need doing as much as they need being, or they remain wishes. Be quiet and call forth one or two of your fondest wishes when you were a girl. What was it? Were you going to be a physician? Have six children? Be wealthy? Be different from your mother? Win an Oscar?

Is that ember still glowing in your soul? The way you give expression to it today will no doubt be different from what you yearned for years ago, but think about how you might channel that energy now, and turn your wish into a dream. As the writer Cheryl Grossman reminds us, "I dream, therefore I become."

The Intuitive Sense

Intuition is a spiritual faculty, and does not explain, but simply points the way.

FLORENCE SCOVEL SHINN

If we are to realize our dreams, it is essential that we use every resource available to us—and intuition is one of the most important tools we've got. Intuition is the capacity to know something without rational evidence that proves it to be so. It is known as the "sixth sense" and is often an ability ascribed to women. The English writer D. H. Lawrence believed that the intelligence that "arises out of sex and beauty is intuition," while anthropologist Margaret Mead concluded that feminine intuition was a result of our "age long training in human relations."

Do you use your intuition? Have you learned how to fine-tune the inner instinct that is constantly transmitting signals to you? Think of yourself as a radio. Is your dial clearly set on the intuitive station so that you can receive its message when you need it, or are you just picking up static?

Intuition is the subliminal sense that Spirit endowed us with to maneuver safely through the maze that is real life. Wild animals rely on their intuition to stay alive; we should rely on ours to thrive. "It is only by following your deepest instinct that you can lead a rich life and if you let your fear of consequence prevent you from following your deepest instinct then your life will be safe, expedient and thin," Katharine Butler Hathaway wrote in 1946.

Intuition tries to communicate with us in inventive ways. One way is through what my friend the script consultant Dona Cooper calls "the educated gut," which frequently slaps us to pay attention by triggering a visceral, physical reaction in our bodies. One such intuitive signal is the emotional trembling that accompanies creative discovery or warns us not to take a certain action. Another intuitive message breaks through when we suddenly grasp that to try something new might be delightful; we do so and are surprised by joy. A third intuitive nudge occurs through revelation, the inner knowing that helps us arrive at the right place at the right time so that we can be swept away by the benevolent flow of synchronicity that gets us where we're meant to be as easily as the Universe can arrange it.

"I believe that we are always attracted to what we need most, an instinct leading us towards the persons who are to open new vistas in our life and fill them with new knowledge," the writer Helen Iswolsky confided in her book *Light before Dusk,* written in 1942. But we've got to be able to follow our intuitive instinct on faith or the new vistas will become voids of despair.

Chapter 1 — Moodlings

Welcome to You

1.   Each one of us makes silent promises to ourselves—to lose ten pounds, begin an exercise program, stop smoking, or some other promise we swear we'll keep. Can you think of some promises you've made to yourself and not kept?

2.   Does the list above look like you've promised yourself with a "have to" or "should do" scolding in mind? Let's try to promise ourselves love. You are dearly loved and deserve to promise yourself joy. How about a ride on the Orient Express, a facial, attending a fashion show of your favorite designer, an aromatherapy massage? What are some promises you can reward yourself with?

3.   How many promises have you made to others and kept at the cost of your own desires? *I'll drive the kids to the pool, I'll make snacks for the soccer team, I'll call you back in a minute.* Think back to yesterday (or last week, or any day that stands out vividly in your mind) and record the promises you made.

4.   Now go back and look at the list of promises above. Which are the ones you're proud of, and which are the ones you feel in retrospect should never have been made? If you allow yourself this kind of analysis every once in a while, I hope you'll find yourself becoming more selective about granting your time to others. The time you do grant will count more now, and you'll feel better about it, and the time you reserve for yourself will feel all the more deserved.

5.   Select one personal promise that you have wanted to keep. When can you keep it? By the end of the month, three months, six months, a year? Record the time frame in the space below. Remember to be realistic—if you are, you're halfway to keeping that promise already.

6.   Let's get cracking at excavating your buried dream. Think about the dreams you've had and abandoned. Now quickly match each dream to the cause of its demise, listed below. This is how we retrace our personal pattern of discouragement.

Good Intentions	*Rejections*
Naïveté (lack of experience)	*Wrong Choices*
Relinquishment	*Bad Timing*
Bitter Failure	*Bungled Efforts*
Detours	*Stupid Mistakes*
Disappointments	*Whims of Fate*

7.   Now think about a dream that you did bring into the world. What action or choice did you do that made this one succeed? If writing down your excavation process feels limiting, work with collage in your Illustrated Discovery Journal. This time look for "concept" pictures—ones that evoke a mood or tell a story. Always remember that your Illustrated Discovery Journal is your Authentic Self's visual autobiography.

8.   Intuition is often described as a "sixth sense," an inner instinct that gives one an instant clarity. You just know. What kinds of things do you use your sixth sense for? Can you sense if something is wrong with a loved one? Do you somehow know ahead of time when someone is going to phone you? Write down some experiences of intuition at work in your life.

Can you think of an instance when your intuition protected you from harm?

9.   Can you think of a time when your intuition nudged you to take a step in a new direction and it enhanced your life in some meaningful way?

10.   How about a time when you didn't listen and an opportunity passed you by?

11.   Make it a priority to hone your intuition. This can easily be achieved through a little practice. The next time you feel a sinking feeling in the pit of your stomach, pay attention. Write it down as soon as you get a chance. How did it turn out? Was the feeling justified? When you get a little feeling of giddiness when faced with another decision, pay attention to that too. If you listened to your instinct, did it pay off?

12.   How does it feel when you honor your intuition, especially if it is uncharacteristic behavior for you? Write down five hunches you have followed in the last week. Look at that list every time you hold back from listening to your own personal cues and remember that a connection with our intuition is a connection to our Authentic Selves.

Write Your Way into Wholeness

You Cannot Fail If You Have Done Your Best, Only If You Have Not Done What You Were Born to Do

They wish to dissuade me
From all that the forces of Love urge me to.
They do not understand it, and I cannot explain it to them.
I must then live out what I am;
What Love counsels my spirit,
In this is my being: for this reason I will do my best.

Hadewijch

Chapter 2

The Fullness of Life

Revelation is the marriage of
knowing and feeling.

MARYA MANNES

There are two insight tools used on the Simple Abundance path that have been catalysts for changing the lives of thousands of people for the better: The Gratitude Journal and the Illustrated Discovery Journal. These were the instruments of grace that turned my life around, so I know for a fact that they were creatively divined and designed to shake up the sensibilities of even the most sophisticated skeptic. Actually what both these journals do for you is reveal what you really love about your life—those elusive gifts now buried beneath the numbing drudgery of unpaid bills, dirty laundry, car repairs, migraine headaches, unceasing work deadlines, and incessant family demands.

At the heart of the Simple Abundance journey is a profound realization: you already possess all you need to be genuinely happy. Today. Not tomorrow or next week or next year. "Do I?" asks a woman on the verge of a nervous breakdown. "Really? Okay, show me the blessings."

Precisely my point.

Gratitude is the most passionate transformative force in the Cosmos. When we offer thanks to God or to

Every time we remember to say "thank you" we experience nothing less than Heaven on earth.

THE SIMPLE
ABUNDANCE
JOURNAL OF
GRATITUDE

another human being, gratitude gifts us with renewal, reflection, reconnection. It is a choice of mind-set—when we put ourselves in a grateful frame of mind, we recognize all the blessings life has granted us.

Once we accept that abundance and lack are parallel realities and that each day we choose—consciously or unconsciously—which world we will inhabit through our attitude, a deep inner shift in our reality occurs. Once during a workshop I was asked to explain the Simple Abundance approach to viewing the world through the prism of a half-empty/half-full glass.

Let's say Abundance is walking down a long, hot, dusty road dying of thirst and along the way she's offered a cold, refreshing glass of water. "Thanks," she says as she drinks it down with gusto. "Bless you. I really needed that." She continues on her way, refreshed and serene, knowing that the next time she needs to quench her thirst, the Universe will be there again, waiting and wanting to supply all her needs.

Lack walks down the same road and when offered the glass of water, hesitantly (what's the catch?) takes a sip. But instead of finishing it, Lack fears that there might not be another pit stop the rest of the journey. So he carries the glass away with him, saving it for when he really needs it later. As he stumbles the water gets hot and undrinkable, spills out of the glass, and eventually begins to evaporate, until there's barely a drop left.

Think about this the next time you drink a glass of water. Where do you come from every day? From abundance or lack?

The Gratitude Journal is a polite, daily thank-you note to the Universe. You know how insulted you are after you've knocked yourself out for your kids and all you get in return is surly silence. What am I raising, you probably wonder, a bunch of brats? Well, an ancient spiritual axiom teaches, "As below, so above."

Because you are not spoiled rotten, at the end of every day you write down five things or moments you've experienced to be grateful for. Small pauses that brought a smile or a sense of relief during the day. Search for the minor as well as the major chords of contentment. Like the kindness of somebody holding your place in the post office line when you have a lot of packages to retrieve from the car. Or when the plumber shows up on time. Fitting into last summer's shorts. A hug from a friend. A fortune cookie with just the right message. Saying no to the bake sale without guilt. Easily switching carpool days. Meeting a deadline. Getting an extension on the deadline. A sigh of relief.

We think it is the big moments that define our lives—the promotion, the new baby, the big house, the engagement. But the narrative of our lives is written in the simple and the small. The big moments are life's punctuation marks.

Several years ago I was invited to teach a Simple Abundance workshop at the Disney Institute in Orlando and my daughter's long-promised, long-awaited trip to Disney World arrived—all expenses paid. One day when I wasn't teaching, I joined Katie and her dad. But the day was cut short by a sudden thunderstorm and it took sev-

All I ask you to do today is to open "the eyes of your eyes" and give your life another glance. . . . Then pause for a moment and give thanks. Let your heart awaken to the transforming power of gratefulness.

SIMPLE ABUNDANCE
JANUARY 13

eral hours for us to make our way back to our hotel. By the time we did, we were all drenched to the skin and chilled to the bone. After hot showers and changing into dry clothes, we went down to the little restaurant in the hotel for a pizza supper. The contented feeling of being warm and dry and happy together was so palpable that they were the first "gifts" I jotted down in my Gratitude Journal that night.

Months later I was flipping through my journal and to my great astonishment saw another entry for that day: *Simple Abundance* hit *USA Today*'s best-seller list for the first time! You would think that this achievement would have been the first entry on my list, but it wasn't. That's because I had learned to appreciate the precious but fleeting little moments in my life—the moments of contentment that truly do make a difference in how you feel, day in, day out. Writing these moments down transforms gratitude from a spiritual sensibility to personal knowledge.

If you give thanks for five gifts every day, in two months you won't look at your life in the same way as you do now. Gratitude can lead you, as it did me, away from the darkness of complicated need into the light of Simple Abundance. In fact, you will not believe what a charmed life you seem to be leading. Why? As the poet Denise Levertov observes, because "That's joy, it's always / a recognition, the know / appearing fully itself, and / more itself than one knew."

Please let me never forget how rich my wonderful life is right at this moment. Please let me never forget that all I have is all I need. Please let me never forget to give thanks.

SIMPLE ABUNDANCE
JULY 1

Interior Vision

*If we go down into ourselves we find
that we possess exactly what we desire.*

SIMONE WEIL

T hose of you who are already familiar (and grateful) for the miracle of harnessing the power of the Universe with just two little words might like to try this new approach with your Gratitude Journal.

Be specific. If you're wrestling with an emotionally charged issue in your life, like money, health, or a relationship, focus your concentration on that issue in a special Gratitude Journal. For instance, let's say you're very worried about money. But it's never the amount of money we have or don't have that's the source of our distress, it's the amount of fear.

Fear is a speculative future-tense emotion. *Will there be enough . . . ? What if there isn't . . . ?* What you really want to do is shift your focus away from your worries about tomorrow's "financial security" to an appreciation of today's "financial serenity." To make that switch, look for ways to thank the Universe for your ever-increasing sense of well-being each day (a friend springs for lunch; the repair bill is less than you imagined; you find $20 in the pocket of a coat you haven't worn for a while; you're thrilled with a thrift-store find) and watch your financial serenity increase steadily, like a savings account. Destiny sketches our life's blueprint with the pencil of our perceptions. Erase the limiting ones.

Some days filling your Gratitude Journal will be easy. Other days—and we all have them—the only thing you might feel thankful for is that the day is over. That's okay, but you still need four more entries, which is why making a master list of your blessings is a reassuring reminder that all you have is all you need. What do you put on your list? Your health, the health of your loved ones. The house or apartment that you're living in, that shelters your dreams—even if it's not your dream house. Don't worry, the dream house will come after gratitude prepares the way for you. What else? How about friendships, work, your favorite meals? The ability to see, to hear, to remember? Jot down ten blessings for your master list right now.

It's okay to repeat some of the same things each day. If you have your health two days in a row, you can (and should) still give thanks for it on the third day.

The recurring acknowledgment of what is working in our lives can help us surmount our difficulties. So consciously give thanks each day for the abundance in your life. When you do you will set in motion an ancient spiritual law: The more you have and are grateful for, the more will be given you. As the months pass and you fill your journal with blessings, focusing on plenty rather than lack, you design a wonderful new blueprint for a simply abundant future.

Begin today. Find a notebook, or a book of beautifully bound empty pages, or *The Simple Abundance Journal of Gratitude* that I published several years ago. Any blank book that pleases you will be fine. Until you get a notebook, jot your blessings down in this book. But your blessings will increase in direct proportion to your awareness of them.

A friend told me that she had decided she was going to move *with* life's energy instead of trying to fight it. In practical terms, if she wanted to remove something heavy from a package she would tilt the package down and let gravity help her. She would do the most difficult aspects of her work in the mornings when her mind was clear and her energy level high, instead of saving those tasks for the end of the day when she was fighting fatigue. She would recommend projects for her company for which there was an enthusiasm of consensus, instead of being the only one committed to a project. She began to move with the Source, or Force, so to speak, and align herself with the creative energy of the Universe. When she did, she began to receive gifts life was offering her—peace of mind, vitality, a sense of accomplishment in place of frustration at work—instead of ignoring them. And the more gifts she noticed, the more she gave thanks.

Soon you'll need more room to record life's gifts than just space in the margins. That's what gratitude does for you; it makes you realize that you don't have to live marginally anymore. Every day is a new blank page!

Being grateful. That's the first step to the path of joy.

SOMETHING MORE
"WHEN THE
STUDENT IS READY"

Self-Gratitude

*Miss Owen and Miss Burney asked me if I had
ever been in love; "with myself," said I, "and most
passionately." When any man likes me I never am
surprised, for I think how should he help it? When
any man does not like me, I think him a blockhead.*

HESTER LYNCH PIOZZI (1781)

Why should self-nurturance be so frightening for most women? Why is it for you? Self-nurturance has been a struggle for me. But believe me, I've learned on the Simple Abundance path that if you want your life to come together, you have to start treating yourself better. One of the ways to do that is by appreciating everything that's right about you and giving thanks for it. Remember the observation of the English poet John Milton: "Good, the more Communicated, more abundant grows."

A pleasurable way to discover what's so abundantly fabulous about yourself is with a personal Self-Gratitude Journal. Or, if you'd prefer, dedicate the last entry in your Gratitude Journal to self-gratitude. Each day you're going to find something wonderful about yourself for which you're grateful. Consider everything. Perhaps it's a new haircut (the one you thought about for so long, and then finally got). Or rising to the occasion with such grace and style when unexpected company came over for dinner. Are you a savvy thrift-store

*We're not meant
to fit in. We're meant
to stand out.*

SOMETHING MORE
"OUR PILGRIMAGE
PLACES"

shopper, an empathetic listener, an inspired cook, a patient and loving mother, a great woman for details? Write it all down.

Self-gratitude, giving thanks for all the good things we are, like self-nurturance is a subtle but very revealing indicator of our self-worth. In fact, these three spiritual graces of *appreciation* (self-gratitude), *action* (self-nurturance), and *acknowledgment* (self-worth) are a woman's personal trinity of transformation.

A Master List of My Blessings

Chapter 2 — Moodlings

The Fullness of Life

1.   Find a notebook, or a book of beautifully bound empty pages, or *The Simple Abundance Journal of Gratitude*. Any blank book that pleases you will be fine. Begin now, writing down five things for which you are grateful today. Record them here if you don't yet have your own Gratitude Journal.

2.   Put down fifty things for your master list.

3.   Think back to the best moments of your life. Moments of clarity and commitment, of transcendence and transformation, exhilaration and engagement. Those moments when you felt so incredibly alive you actually offered thanks without prompting.

   What are the first memories that come to mind?

4.   We are going to acknowledge and honor our authentic gifts. What first comes to mind when you think of *your* natural talents?

5.   Now, what are your fondest wishes for yourself? Can you match each to a gift that can help make yur wishes come true?

6.   What are some unlikely sources of inspiration you've had, and what in particular touched you?

7.   How good are you at recognizing gratitude in others? Are there certain signs—a smile, a touch of a hand—that let you know when someone is truly grateful for an act of kindness that you, or someone else, has sent their way? Do you incorporate these signs and signals into your own life, so that others may recognize what makes *you* grateful, and send more blessings your way?

8.   Make a gift continuum. Go from the most frivolous of purchases (a piece of jewelry with stones on the inside, so that only *you* know they are there) to the more practical (a session with a closet organizer) to the intangible (kindness, clarity of vision)—all things you wish you had. Study the list. Are there patterns in what you desire? What are you learning about the nature of your wishes?

Write Your Way into Wholeness

You Do Not Serve Spirit Well by Playing Small

Risk! Risk anything! Care no more for the opinions of others,
for those voices. Do the hardest thing on earth for you.
Act for yourself. Face the truth.

Katherine Mansfield

Chapter 3

Romancing the Soul

She had been forced into prudence in her youth.
She learned romance as she grew older—
the natural sequence of an unnatural beginning.

JANE AUSTEN

Plumb the female psyche and you will find an elegy of romantic remorse—for the unobtained, the undone. Regrets for the things we loved once but learned to live without. It could be the novel you abandoned writing, the art fellowship in Paris you never pursued, the black velvet cape that finally found you at an antique stall but you passed up because where would you wear it? (everywhere). The love you couldn't return, the love that frightened you, the love that you were afraid to express. The loving gesture that died in hesitation. The romance of living that we let slip away every day because real life forces us into prudence.

When you acknowledge your romantic impulses, no matter how implausible or impractical (I had a friend who bought an extraordinarily inappropriate white rabbit coat that made her deliriously happy), you strengthen the intimate connection with your Authentic Self. The connection with those who cherish and love you unconditionally. The connection with those things that fuel your passions, feed your soul, keep you alive.

Begin today, exploring small ways in which to honor your sacred yearning for romance.

Your Paper Soul Mate

*Like any art, the creation of self is both
natural and seemingly impossible.
It requires training as well as magic.*

HOLLY NEAR

The Gratitude Journal roots you into your present, offering moments of comfort, glimmers of joy, and a deep awareness of the "simple abundance" that surrounds you daily. The second essential insight tool for our year together on the path to authenticity is the Illustrated Discovery Journal.

Sometimes in order to believe in yourself, you need someone else to continually believe in you, for you, with you, despite you—force-feeding you faith, like an intravenous drip. Someone to confide in, someone you can trust completely, someone who understands you better than you understand yourself. Someone who isn't afraid of your passion but excited by it. Someone who realizes that what you call your weaknesses may actually be your hidden strengths. Someone who does not get frustrated, exasperated, annoyed, or incredulous at anything you do, because she loves you unconditionally. She's your Authentic Self, and you'll enjoy a secret rendezvous with this fabulous gal pal on the pages of the Illustrated Discovery Journal.

The Illustrated Discovery Journal accelerates the

*Gradually, as you
become curator of your
own contentment, you
will learn to embrace
the gentle yearnings of
your heart.*

SIMPLE ABUNDANCE
JANUARY 1

34

unfolding of the authentic journey through pure intuition and feeling. When you collect random pictures that appeal to you—images culled from periodicals or cut out of catalogs, photographs, or postcards—and reflectively assemble them into collages, your paper soul mate will reveal just about anything you might ever want to know about yourself. Your passions. Your preferences. What tickles you. What ticks you off. What makes you happy.

To conjure up your paper soul mate, you will need a blank artist's sketchbook or *The Illustrated Discovery Journal* I created to accompany this workbook. You'll also need magazines, catalogs, and paper ephemera from which you'll be cutting and pasting your authentic clues. When you are in a relaxed, receptive state, flip through the magazines, and when an image jumps off the page, cut it out and later paste it in your journal. Even if you are mostly concerned with how you want to liven up your bedroom, or your wardrobe, the images that speak to you can and should be wide-ranging (for example, a sandy beach or cool green forest; a colorful, inviting table setting; children making valentines; photos of galaxies in space). In my own Illustrated Discovery Journal I have also added quotes, sketches, newspaper photos, greeting cards, postcards, travel brochures, and pressed flowers.

If you find that you are wrestling with a very difficult problem—whether to accept a new job, have a child, move to another town—and the solution is not evident, go through magazines or mail-order catalogs and look for images. Just cut them out, and put them together in a collage as you think about whatever you're struggling with. It's no wonder that psychotherapists often use collage as a tool to help their patients process difficult issues.

Don't try to arrange the pictures in any specific order; let the collages you are creating simply evolve. Soon they will give you direction about where your heart wants to go. You'll feed your imagination and get in touch with your authenticity by gathering together beautiful images that speak to your soul. This might be pictures of cabbage roses or of a gleaming black Labrador; a beautiful oriental rug; a couple on the beach. A view from a window. A woman playing a harp in a mysterious-looking room. Clouds in the sky.

Sometimes we are cut off from knowing what it is we love. We have lost touch. So let's be inner explorers, seeking adventure and our own unknown. Authentic archaeologists know how to unearth remnants of memory buried deeply in the fertile soil of the subconscious mind. Archaeologists "read" artifacts much the way a detective reads clues.

Close your eyes and visualize your ideal life. Now see how you live and who lives with you. What does your dream house look like? What part of the country is it in? Do you have children? What type of garden do you have? Is there water nearby? Do you have a dog or other pets? What kind of job do you have, what kind of car? Record here what is in your picture:

Now see if you can find pictures in magazines to match your ideal ones.

Think fun. Think seven years old. This is a wish list to the Universe. Our deepest wishes are whispers of our authentic selves. I believe that everything is created in our minds before it manifests itself in the outer world. We must believe it before we can see it. When searching for buried treasure, you have to know what you're digging for, before *X* can mark the spot.

Find a photograph of yourself, from when you were about ten years old. Put a photocopy of it in your Illustrated Discovery Journal. Send love to that young girl. Travel back in time and imagination. See yourself at ten: at home, at school, in the neighborhood. Where did you live?

Do a mental walk-through of the rooms of your childhood home and see them once again. How were they decorated? What did your bedroom look like? Did you keep your room clean or messy? Was the door usually kept closed? What was your favorite spot in the house? Was your mother a good cook? Do you ever prepare any of her special recipes? How did your mother *comfort* you when you were sick? Who were your friends? How did you play? Where did you go on vacation? Are there sense memories you associate with childhood vacations? The smell of eucalyptus, or pine trees? Cold, clear lake water, German pancakes in a black frying pan sizzling over a campfire? Sleeping in a sleeping bag, near huge granite rocks? What do you remember?

Now fast-forward to your teenage years. Who in your class did you admire, or envy? Who initiated you into the feminine rituals of good grooming? Was there an older woman in your life whose sense of style impressed you?

Take a blank page in your Illustrated Discovery Journal and create a one-page autobiography of yourself as a child. Make it multimedia, using visual images from magazines or your own drawings as well as words. Place the images first and then see what written thoughts want to accompany them.

Ten was probably the last time you trusted your instincts. Try to contact the girl you once were. She's all grown up now. She is your Authentic Self and she's waiting to remind you how beautiful, accomplished, and extraordinary you really are.

Leave the collage for three days. Three is a very mystical, powerful number in many cultures. Give your conscious mind a time out. Let your heart mull over the images and your soul can reveal the authentic answer. Come back to the collage three days later and see what it tells you.

Telling Your Story

*I am not at all the sort of person
you and I took me for.*

JANE WELSH CARLYLE

Mary McCarthy said, "We are the hero of our own story." I want you to start to think that way: You are the heroine of your own story.

When you view yourself as the heroine of your own story, you are given the ability to look at yourself from a safe distance. "The eyes of your eyes" as the story-teller become open; you're not judging yourself or your choices, because this is the stuff of drama.

I think this is what we need to do to reclaim our lives. Recast them as stories. That's what you're doing with your words and pictures, creating a visual memoir.

You might think you are not a natural storyteller, or that writing stories does not come easily to you. But as you begin to record your own stories regularly through images, you'll be amazed at how much you start remembering or recognizing. Recording your stories does not have to mean sitting down for hour upon hour writing slavishly all the memories that come to mind. No, it sim-

*The key to loving
how you live is in
knowing what it
is you truly love.*

SIMPLE ABUNDANCE
JANUARY 28

39

ply means you should jot things down when you get a glimmer of insight—when you're cutting up vegetables, washing dishes, brushing your teeth. Just note things so that you don't forget them, and the narrative will begin to pull itself together. The work knows more than you do. You're just the storyteller, the conduit.

For years I collected the catalogs of J. Peterman. He illustrated his products with beautiful watercolor drawings, and described them richly, colorfully. One day I selected some of his descriptive words and phrases to define myself—as another way of telling my own story. At the end of this chapter I've listed some of my favorites. Which of these most apply to you?

One of Peterman's lines says, "You know her better than yourself, except when you don't know her at all. A wind sweeping through every part of your life, rearranging even the past. Who is this woman?"

Well, you're going to find out. You can paste these words around a picture of yourself, or you can just put them in your Illustrated Discovery Journal.

If you don't have a picture of yourself that you like now, get one taken that you do like. It doesn't have to be professional; you can do this with a friend. Just get an inexpensive camera, or a disposable one, and take pictures. Have them developed, see which ones call to you, and put them in your Illustrated Discovery Journal.

Here is another way of telling your story: In a wonderful little book called *A Creative Companion: How to Free Your Creative Spirit,* SARK asks the reader to "Write a portrait or description of your 'ideal self.' Make it glow.

Reveal all your best qualities. Start with 'I am.'" Follow her instructions, but rather than make the story too long, keep it to no more than two pages, or five hundred words.

You can begin here:

I am

Telling my own stories to myself has always been my homeopathic remedy. Each story, usually in the form of a daydream, starred my own romantic heroine, an extraordinary woman who triumphed over her travails with courage, grace, and grit. This woman was beautiful and radiant; she reflected, even in the worst situations, the essential characteristics of all romantic heroines—repose of the soul. *She was my Authentic Self—my soul made visible.*

But I needed, as you will, time and space to grow into my authenticity and to accept myself—not for what is wrong, but for what is gloriously right.

The wonderful writer Kennedy Fraser was once in a period of her life that she calls her "armchair period," a detour of dormancy that strikes every spiritual journey. Dormancy visits all of us, but our fallow time can take place as we are lying in bed or standing in front of the refrigerator. Fraser was encouraged by reading other women's stories, which "seemed to stretch out a hand" that helped pull her through her abyss.

Other women's stories also helped pull me back to the safety of my own sanity.

We can learn from the stories of other women, especially women who change their images and lifestyles to reflect their authenticity. Sometimes these makeovers are called "reinventing." I call it evolution. Don't think, "If I reinvent myself, I'm not true to who I really am." Instead, I say you've never been more *faithful!* What you're doing is shedding other people's image of who you are, so that the new skin of your Authentic Self is visible.

And you thought you were just coloring your hair!

The Inner Witch

Cruelty is the only sin.

ELLEN GLASGOW

I don't know about your inner critic, but I see mine as Cruella de Vil, the evil villainess in *101 Dalmatians* played by Glenn Close. Cruella de Vil in all Glenn Close's glory is what my inner critic looks like. In order to finally silence her I needed to replace the image in my imagination, and so I invited Agatha Christie's Miss Marple to pay a visit.

When I first began working on *Simple Abundance,* I realized that I had to become a detective of my own life. In this role, I would experience a profound shift in perspective; a detective doesn't bring judgment to the scene of the crime. A detective simply looks for clues, gathers information, makes connections, puts it all together. I wanted to look at my life this way, to find its patterns and priorities. I also wanted to silence the inner critical voice that was constantly telling me I wasn't good enough, that I wasn't doing things perfectly enough.

So the first place I started to look for clues was my calendar, and what I noticed was that there was time in it for everybody except myself. When you start to introduce self-nurturance into your life, which is fundamental to the journey of self-discovery, one of the first things you do is to try to carve out a little time for yourself. Most women I know are terminally exhausted because we are careaholics.

We care for our husbands, our partners, our children. We care for our siblings, our parents, our friends. We care about our work, our jobs. We care about the church rummage sale. We care about political and social issues. We care about everything. The only thing we don't care about is ourselves. We know that when push comes to shove, we easily push aside our own needs in order to take care of others.

When I looked at my calendar and realized that there was no space in the day, week, or month for me to take care of my needs, I was shocked. Like most women,

I was incapable of saying no. We think that if we say no, people are not going to like us. So before we know it, all the things we've said yes to fill our calendars to the brim and our days with quiet desperation.

So I had to be clever. I had to realize that the same intelligence that had gotten me into this mess could get me out. I took a yellow marker and just highlighted two hours a week for myself on my calendar, but I didn't put my name in. I didn't identify this time as SBB's because I knew if I saw the time was "just my own" I would cross out my name and put someone else's in. So I let the yellow highlighted time block become a subliminal connection. This way if I was asked to do something I could easily say, "You know, I'd like to but I can't, I have another commitment." And I did—to myself.

I began to call these two-hour periods "creative excursions," which you take with your best gal pal—the Authentic Self. For what is the first gift we bring to any new love relationship? It is the most precious of gifts: our time. When we *want* to be with somebody we always find the time.

Be as generous in your relationship with your Authentic Self. Start by giving both of you two hours a week to do whatever it is you want to do. You can just sit and hear yourself think if you want to. Please choose a lovely, comfy spot!

In addition to gifting ourselves with time, we need to bless ourselves with a nurturing touch. In *Simple Abundance* I wrote about Mother's Day (May 13), reflecting that many women I know still yearn to be comforted, to be mothered. Though we are adults, we never outgrow the need for someone special to hold us close, stroke our hair, tuck us into bed, and reassure us that tomorrow all will be well.

We may need to reacquaint ourselves with the maternal and deeply comforting dimension of Divinity, in order to learn how to mother ourselves. And the best way to start is to create, as an act of worship, a comfortable home that protects, nurtures, and sustains all who come there—including you!

Consider how you can start to mother yourself—every day, not just once a year—in small but tangible ways. There should be *comfortable places* from the living room to the bedroom that invite you to sit, sleep, relax, and reflect. There should be small indulgences from the kitchen to the bathroom that pamper and please. There should be sources of beauty throughout that inspire. Where can you create places and touches of comfort? Walk around your home now. Jot down any immediate ideas.

Living with Flowers and Herbs

*Arranging a bowl of flowers in the morning
can give a sense of quiet in a crowded day—
like writing a poem, or saying a prayer.*

ANNE MORROW LINDBERGH

As I got more in touch with my authentic preferences and sought joyful simplicities to brighten up my daily round, I realized how much I longed to be surrounded by the visual beauty of Spirit expressed in Nature. The newly discovered sensualist in me wanted feasts for the eyes and sweet scents for my home.

The famous English gardener and writer Vita Sackville-West believed that gardening was like painting. You can create a fresh, beautiful canvas with the pinks, blues, purples, reds, and whites of flowers, whether in an outdoor garden or a vase inside your home; the profusion of color can be so intoxicating as to make you swoon.

Living with flowers is an exquisite, simple pleasure. In the spring, summer, and fall it is an affordable luxury. People have been decorating their homes with "botanicals" for over 4,500 years, as evidenced by Egyptian wall paintings. Interior florals can make a garden bloom indoors.

If you're having a hard time realizing the garden

that lives inside your heart, there is a way to express it, if there's a desire. Bring plants into your home. Consider fragrant ones redolent of romance: camellias, freesias, narcissus, hyacinths, heliotrope, jasmine, violets, scented geraniums.

A fragrant home is a simple pleasure, but one rich in the resonance of reassurance. Subtly layering scents throughout the rooms in your home imparts a feeling of luxury to your living spaces. Air out your rooms. Use pine cleansers and lemon-scented furniture polish.

For centuries in Benedictine cloisters, gardening—particularly herb gardening—has been considered an important ritual in the daily round of religious life. But the devotion to growing herbs can be traced back nearly six thousand years before the Christian era. In ancient civilizations like those of Egypt, China, and Assyria, herbalists were revered. There is probably more mystery and lore to herbs than any other plants. Each herb has its own history, significance, and use either in cooking or remedies.

Take a creative excursion to a farmer's market or a spice and herb shop. Delight in the simple pleasure of your sense of smell. Indulge yourself with comforting aromas. Gather aromatic herb plants—rosemary, tarragon, thyme, bay, and fresh lavender.

Put out bowls of fragrant potpourri; simmer apple cider, cinnamon, and cloves in water on your stove.

The world around us possesses exquisite smells that can stir our memories, color our emotions, and

Passion is part of Real Life's package—we were created by Love, for love, to love. If we're unsure of our passions we must continue excavating until we rediscover them, for if we don't give outward expression to our passions in little ways every day, we will eventually experience self-immolation— the spontaneous combustion of our souls.

SOMETHING MORE
"SELF-IMMOLATION"

transform our feelings and moods. Once when I was sitting on a porch with a dear friend who was dying, she said to me, "Oh, I love the fragrance of newly cut grass, don't you?" It was one of the last times she savored that simple pleasure. Today, when you inhale something wonderful, offer a prayer of thanksgiving for this marvelous gift and your ability to receive it.

Red-Flag Fantasies

If one is lucky a solitary fantasy can totally transform one million realities.

MAYA ANGELOU

In *Simple Abundance* I described a common fantasy of women—a red-flag warning—having to do with an overwhelming impulse to disappear one day without a trace. I call this fantasy "Scrambled or Fried." Suddenly you can't take it anymore; you just want to run away, to begin life all over again somewhere where nobody knows your name and nobody can yank your chain. Perhaps in the West as a waitress in a diner. You have no more stress—all you have to do is ask your customers if they'd like their eggs scrambled or fried.

What are your favorite red-flag fantasies? Is one of them about escape? About slamming the door shut and beginning a new life? Are your fantasies about fame? Sex? Love? Money? Glamour? List them:

When my best friend and I were teenagers, we would plot how the next time we were mad at our parents we were going to run away from home. "Then they'll be sorry!" we said. The trouble was, we were never mad at our parents at the same time, so we never ran away. Although there was great clarity about how we would take money and clothes and a suitcase and sneak out of the house, there was a vagueness about where we were headed. This fuzziness regarding the details of escape still occurs for many women who feel stuck in their circumstances but can't seem to make a change.

As crazy as this seems, I think it's easier for women to think of quitting their jobs or leaving their marriages than to actually take a day off! So in acting on our fantasies let's start with the courageous act of taking a real day off. Running around taking care of a month's worth of errands instead of showing up at the office does not count. What does? You get a massage, take a walk, get some exercise, go to a lecture, enroll in a workshop. You contact an old friend. Whatever it is, it should be something that breaks a pattern and opens up a new vista.

Contemplating a plan of escape is an imaginary mechanism to let off steam from life's pressure cooker. How can you "run away" without actually doing it?

Recognizing Burnout

All extremes are dangerous.

VIRGINIA WOOLF

Accepting uncreative days as part of the creative cycle is crucial to your serenity. Uncreative days are real life. Every artist knows them. Uncreative days are the part of the yin and yang of artistic yearning. Who do we think we are, expecting to be creative and productive every day of our lives? Just look at Nature, in which there are periods of growth and times for lying fallow.

When you're in a creative drought you still have to go through the motions and keep showing up for work. Your assignment is to replenish the well. Search for the underground spring through creative excursions and through exercise, yoga, healthy eating, sleep. When I'm deeply discouraged, I retreat to my Illustrated Discovery Journal, searching for visual clues to indicate the next turn in the path. Or leap into the future.

In the natural world, droughts depart as suddenly and mysteriously as they arrive. The writer Etty Hillesum reminds us, "One must also accept that one has 'uncreative' moments. The more honestly one can accept that the quicker these moments will pass. One must have the courage to call a halt, to feel empty and discouraged."

Life is supposed to be a romantic adventure.

SOMETHING MORE
"FACING YOUR
FUTURE BY
EXCAVATING
YOUR PAST"

The hardest thing we'll do as artists of the everyday is to learn to call an occasional halt and release the pressure on ourselves.

A friend who is a book editor knew she was burned out; she recognized that, in her case, the salt had indeed lost its savor. What she wanted was a sabbatical, but you can't do that easily in the publishing industry. It's not like teaching—they'll go on without you, and you may not have a job to come back to! So my friend struggled on. In the manner of a creative editor, though, she realized that there was potential for a popular book on the subject of burnout: how to recognize it, how to cure it. It didn't fully cure her own burnout, but at least she was able to make creative use of what was happening to her and learn a bit more about herself at the same time.

Burnout is a condition caused by unbalance: too much work or responsibility, too little time to do it, over too long a period.

When have you felt burned out, and how have you addressed the problem? What else could/can you do?

Sometimes burnout manifests itself in a sense of complete exhaustion at the end of a project that has taken months of challenging and intense work. Taking a week off to rest, then resuming work at a slower pace, is usually enough to bring about a speedy recovery. But first-degree burnout—the soul snuffer—comes from living an unbalanced life for years; when what was supposed to be a temporary situation becomes a lifestyle.

Burnout often begins with illness and is usually accompanied by depression. It's burnout when you feel trapped and hopeless, unable to dream, experience pleasure, or find contentment. Something is terribly out of whack: you.

Rituals of self-nurturance are the mortar that holds the day together. Treating yourself well on the job can serve as a source of inspiration to bring out your best. When starting a new project, ask yourself, "Is there anything I can do to make this task more pleasurable?" If there is, do it. Working happier accomplishes much more than working harder.

Think about affordable luxuries when you think about nurturing your personal style. What simple pleasures could make you feel more abundant?

Learn to create ceremonies of personal pleasure that can nourish your deeper longings. As you nurture your spirit with kindness, your physical cravings for things that aren't good for you—for chocolate, cigarettes, alcohol—will loosen their grip.

Just as negative addictions sneak up on us a day at a time, so do positive cravings. Meditation, creative movement, moments of self-nurturance that bring contentment—all can become positive habits of well-being. I find that when I take twenty minutes to get quiet and go within, work with the visual images in my Illustrated Discovery Journal, take a walk, or ask how I can make the next task more pleasurable, my wants diminish.

Chapter 3 — Moodlings

Romancing the Soul

1.   Today, make a list of ten nice things you could do for yourself.

2.   If you could go anywhere in the world, all expenses paid, baby-sitter at your disposal, where would you go? Paris? Beijing? Istanbul? Mexico? Santa Fe? Charleston? Why? Who would you be with? What would you do?

3.   What emotional talismans do you treasure? These, or representations of them, are the items that will go in your Illustrated Discovery Journal. Do you cherish a family photograph? An heirloom clock? Pressed flowers, dancing shoes, a special tree? Love letters? A trophy, a diploma, a good review? List some of these benchmarks:

4.   When filling your Illustrated Discovery Journal with pictures that trigger an emotional response (even if you don't understand why), you are remembering things long forgotten. We know them, it's just that we have forgotten them. It's that way with any kind of dream.

We're going to go back so that you can take another look at a dream, small or large, that you may have abandoned. What might this be?

5.   What are your favorite sensual memories? What can bring back today, with a rush, a full-blown, enveloping memory? For me it is the smell of Irish peat moss burning in a fireplace, the feel of the fog creeping over the hills, the sound of a first Christmas carol. And for you?

6.   What did you love and notice in your favorite books? The heroines? Background details? Stories? Which heroine did you love in *Little Women*? What are the qualities that you loved?

A wonderful resource for this exercise is *Once Upon a Heroine: 400 Books for Girls to Love*, edited by Alison Cooper-Mullin and Jennifer Marmaduke Coye. Remember you're never too old to read the books you missed as a girl!

Are any of these threads incorporated into your life today? If so, how?

7.   Contemplating a plan of escape is an imaginary mechanism to let off steam from life's pressure cooker. How can you "run away" without actually doing it? Try to come up with seven "runaway" days—if you've gone years without one, one week's worth shouldn't be too hard to imagine!

8.   Now that you have a list, work up the courage, break out your rigid schedule, and take one. What did you do? How did it feel? Writing down these feelings will help them last longer, and help you to seek them out in daily living.

9.   Are you having an uncreative day? Here's a lighthearted exercise that can help. Think of your favorite superheroine or comic strip character. Is it Wonder Woman? Batgirl? Cathy? Spend some time looking at your day through her eyes. What do you observe? At best, this will show you a different take on the problems that face you and might help you solve them, and at worst, it's good for a laugh—and we should never underestimate the value of a good laugh!

10.   In my workshop we call this exercise "Self-Centered." Photocopy these phrases, cut them out, and paste the phrases that describe your Authentic Self around your favorite photograph of yourself. Don't hold back. Now is the time to get the sassy praise you've always deserved!

Oh Yes

The Road Not Taken

Companion

Writer

True Glam

Prosperous-Looking

God Bless Us

DIRECTOR

Glamour

Security

No Regrets

Wild Style

Back to Nature

Amazing Grace

A Dangerous Woman

The New Look

How Does She Do It?

Touchable

Portrait of a Lady

Guess Who

Pretty Smart

The Simple Life

Grown-Up Fun

WINNING TICKET

. . . A Little Imagination

Right This Way

People Will Listen

AUTHENTIC

Friendly

Best Friend

The Right Stuff

First-Class

Write Your Way into Wholeness

Nourish Your Beginnings As You Would a Baby

Nourish beginnings, let us nourish beginnings
Not all things are blest, but the
Seeds of all things are blest.
The blessing is in the seed.

Muriel Rukeyser

Chapter 4

Phenomenal Woman

One can never consent to creep
when one feels an impulse to soar.

HELEN KELLER

The monarch butterfly has an uncanny sense of place, a genetic code carried within its being that is passed down through five generations. No matter where it is hatched it can find its way back 2,500 miles to the place of its ancestral origins, a place it has never been before.

So do we. Our soul's sense of place is our authenticity. But we don't arrive there on a straight path. Just as the butterfly flits from side to side as she flies, we flit and flirt with fortune on our way to finding ourselves. However, before the butterfly soars, she undergoes a process very like reembodiment.

I have a friend who is an expert on butterflies, and she creates butterfly gardens. She explained to me what happens when a caterpillar begins the transfiguration process toward her authenticity. Before the caterpillar starts the process she eats and eats and eats and eats and that's all she does for days. Then she'll climb up on some kind of slanted stick or a root with a pointed end that's stretching upward toward infinity. Slowly she creeps. Slowly, slowly, slowly. When she gets to the top, probably thinking, "Whew," her life's work is just begun. For now she begins to weave a silk thread that will hold her to the stick like a bungee cord. Next she spins the silk thread around herself to create a sacred place—the chrysalis—in which to sleep. While she's sleeping Mother Nature deconstructs her form and the caterpillar undergoes a transformation; her body completely breaks down and is turned to liquid. From this watery substance a butterfly takes form, and when the transformation is complete she breaks through, a completely new being. Her true self.

Each of us has an authentic style, and we manifest it in our appearance, in the way we decorate, the way we arrange flowers, the way we cook. We manifest it in every choice we make because we are artists of the everyday. I believe that authentic style is a gift of Spirit, and that when we celebrate who we are, Spirit blesses us and we become women of Substance, Style, and Spirit.

There is no one in the world just like you. Do you know that yet? Nobody can express Divinity in the way that you do every day. Some days you might express it more colorfully, with more joy and passion than on other days—that's okay. But we all have those extraordinary moments when we feel truly alive, when we're just bursting with happiness, and we're going to try to bring more of those moments into your daily round.

When you take the path to authenticity, you start taking risks in ways that you never could before. Risks spiritually induce reembodiment.

My first two books were written about Victoriana,

Let's shed our outmoded attitudes about what's fashionable, and replace them with new ideas about what works for us in our real lives and truly reflects our authenticity.

SIMPLE ABUNDANCE
MARCH 25

and I gave workshops based on those books and dressed as if I were a Victorian woman. By the time I was writing *Simple Abundance* I had stopped doing those workshops, and yet my personal style was still lace-trimmed frills and the big Gibson girl hair of the Victorian era.

Most of the time I felt uncomfortable in my own skin, as if I were a ghost inhabiting someone else's body. I wanted desperately to move on, but I didn't know how. But as I started working with my Illustrated Discovery Journal, cutting images out of magazines and mail-order catalogs, visceral visual images began to speak to me. When I listened to them I realized that all the women I selected were dressed simply. Sparsely. Streamlined. My interior vision was paring down, but I didn't realize this until I started to see a pattern.

When you start putting images into your Illustrated Discovery Journal, make no value judgments. Only choose something because it speaks to you. Later, after you finish a collage, you'll be able to translate its message. Make changes with baby steps. When I started this process I was wearing my hair long, and gradually I had it cut shorter. I was experimenting. I was so hungry to find myself that I was willing to experiment because I figured, what the heck, it can always grow back. (And it can!)

You're not going to change your look or your home overnight. You're not meant to. This is a slow process. Just as when you're pregnant with a child, from the moment you conceive that child it takes nine months until birth; in a sense, you are giving birth to a new you here, and like the baby or the butterfly, it deserves its own gestation period. Begin as I did with simple questions about yourself. "Who is she? What does she love?"

I have never been athletic, other than doing horseback riding. But a few summers ago I had the chance to go whitewater rafting. It was one of those "what the heck" moments I've come to relish. Well, it was terrifying! But after it was over and I realized I had survived it, I felt exhilarated, and very much alive. Next came hiking. I'm looking forward to riding in a hot-air balloon and learning to scuba dive.

We can take small risks, in how we express ourselves—through our clothing, through our accessories, through simple gestures. Have you been dressing most of your life so that you will blend in, not stand out? So that you can hide even from yourself?

Celebrate a New Beauty

The beauty that addresses itself to the eyes is only the spell of the moment; the eye of the body is not always that of the soul.

GEORGE SAND

Think about all the people in your life, women and men, who are the most successful, the most kind, the most intelligent, the most confident, the most in love, the most happy. Do they fit our culture's image of what is most beautiful? Odds are against it. So why do you think you have to conform to that impossible standard in order to possess those wonderful qualities? You don't.

In her book *Love Your Looks,* psychotherapist Carolynn Hillman suggests imagining five new planets: Darkhairland, Shortland, Roundland, Ageland, and Thinland. Each one has a distinct model of beauty. On Darkhairland, for example, only women with the blackest hair are considered attractive; on Roundland, thin women are ridiculed, while on Thinland, women have been known to starve themselves to death in pursuit of the ideal appearance. Then Hillman takes us to Multi-Pleasureland. This is a place where women of every size, shape, color, and age are considered beautiful, where differences are celebrated, not shunned.

Where would you like to live?

This exercise illustrates how arbitrary society's beauty standards are. Understanding this allows you to expand your idea of beauty—to include yourself.

The Woman You're Meant to Be

One is not born, but rather becomes a woman.

SIMONE DE BEAUVOIR

The Authentic Self is waiting to help you evolve into the woman you were meant to become. An easy way to let her begin is while you're working on your Illustrated Discovery Journal. Flip through the different mail-order catalogs you have gathered and cut out pictures of the women you think are attractive and the clothing you'd love to wear. Don't worry about cost—this is a creative brainstorming session. Remember that dreams—your creative visualizations—always come before physical manifestations.

Create a collage of your ideal woman—her wardrobe, her hairstyle. Pretend you're ten years old and playing with paper dolls. Does anything in your Illustrated Discovery Journal collage resemble anything hanging in your closet?

Now make yourself a promise. Since you have embarked on this adventure to awaken your authenticity and discover your own sense of style, be willing to not buy another item of clothing unless you absolutely cannot live without it (an old friend of mine, a wise woman, once said this is the only way to buy a house as well—only if you cannot sleep at night for wanting it). No more settling for something that "will do," or that's not you, or that's second-rate.

On the Simple Abundance path you're going to discover the joy of surrounding yourself only with things you love, and the pleasure of wearing only clothes that make you look and feel fabulous and project your authentic sense of style (whether jeans and a T-shirt in a color that matches your eyes or a shimmery cocktail dress that accents your gorgeous hourglass figure). If something isn't authentically you, it's liberating to live without it.

By now I hope you have discovered wonderful features about your own face and body. Each of us has at least one special feature that can set us apart. Do you accentuate your assets? It has been said that the secret to a Frenchwoman's beauty is knowing what her real asset is—eyes, lips, long legs, small waist—and that she highlights that feature, whether with eye shadow, lipstick, well-fitted skirts, wide belts, or a scarf tied just so. What are *your* best features?

Simplicity plays a part in striking the right chord. This occurs naturally as we begin to rethink how to put together our signature look. Gradually we learn that authentic style applies to makeup and fashion as well as to decorating and entertaining. As we go within, searching for spiritual growth, we begin to blossom on the outside. You just cannot start spiritual transformation and not see it reflected on the outside. With spiritual truth, what is true within is true without. What is hidden will be revealed.

Let's shed our outmoded attitudes about what's fashionable and replace them with new ideas about what works for us in our real lives. What if everything hanging in your closet were something you loved, some-

We should only strive to be a first-rate version of ourselves. And our best is always good enough.

SIMPLE ABUNDANCE
MARCH 23

thing that made you look beautiful or made you feel wonderful when you put it on? Think of how good you would feel every day.

So divest yourself of clothing you *don't* want, to make room for things you do want. Clear away the fashion clutter of past incarnations that lurks in your closets. Just because you bought it once doesn't mean you have to keep it forever. Be willing to let simplicity pare down your wardrobe to your authentic essence. Identify the clothes you absolutely love and can't imagine living without:

Edit your fashion accessories as well as your clothes (do this when you feel and look good; put on makeup and do your hair). Keep *only* those things that you would mourn if you lost them.

Consider the various real lives you lead and the clothes you need for them in three categories: work, dress-up, and comfort. If you haven't worn something in a year, why not? Be willing to part with it even if it was expensive. Ask yourself if an item makes you feel fabulous and beautiful or confident and comfortable; they are the ones to keep. Imagine the joy of opening your closet in the morning and finding nothing but clothes that fit that description!

I am convinced that we are our own best selves in comfort clothes. Somehow, through the alchemy of fiber and fit, we are once again restored to Paradise. We go back again to when we were ten years old and could climb trees and run like the wind.

You can give old clothes away; or if you still love them but can't wear them, give them to your daughter, your niece, a friend's daughter (and Daughter, Niece, if you receive such a gift, say *thank you!*). Or you can recycle these wonderful fabrics—by making a rug or a quilt, for example.

This month, be ruthless. Examine closely the items you reach for in your wardrobe when in need of comfort. *Look for clues to help you bring more comfort into your life.* The Simple Abundance path encourages us to be patient until we find what's perfect for us.

As with any of the arts, a sense of style is one that needs to be nurtured after it is initially divined and devised. Style begins when you seek and discover your strengths, then bank on them for all they're worth. Personal style flourishes when you realize that you don't need as much clothing, accessories, jewelry, or makeup as you once thought you did, because you've got attitude.

In searching for your authenticity you will uncover your own signature look. This month, be willing to experiment to find out what works for you and what doesn't.

Pass Not Unnoticed

Fashion can be bought. Style one must possess.

EDNA WOOLMAN CHASE

Elegance is the art of restraint. Famous, wealthy women known for their chic sense of style keep their looks uncluttered. Elegance in personal style requires only that a woman major in the classics: comfort, color, shape, fabric, value, and appropriateness. Elegance means that clothes never eclipse the woman within but permit her inner light to shine. Perhaps the soul of elegance is a "simply abundant" state of mind.

In the 1970s it was all the rage to have your colors done, which meant matching your own skin, eye, and hair color to a prescribed color palette from which you would then choose clothing and accessories that best suited you. This was helpful, but it wasn't foolproof.

Consider the role that color plays in your life. To build a wardrobe with staying power, invest in classic colors for the foundation—black, white, navy, gray, beige, camel, tan, khaki, ivory, and the "reds," including wine and russet. With classic colors, your wardrobe gradually grows and never goes out of style. Now punctuate your personal style with accent colors that you adore and that look best on you—like rose, or yellow, or green.

How do you find your best colors? Experiment and study yourself in the mirror. Finally, never underestimate the power of love. Trust your instincts. It took me a while to pay attention to the fact that if I *smiled* in an outfit I was trying on in the store, I should probably buy it.

You can use color to express your many moods. Today think about the colors you love. This week take a creative excursion to a paint store and look at the color spectrum. What are the colors that speak to your soul? Pick up some chips. Next, go to a fabric store and find a pattern that catches your eye. Buy a yard of it. Drape it over a couch or pin it up on a wall. Live with the colors for a month, then make the fabric into a pillow and paint a room or a piece of furniture in your new hue.

We want to feel comfortable in our own skin, we want to wear clothes that induce that feeling, or that we feel beautiful in. What are three items of clothing that make you feel beautiful? A fluffy pink sweater? Yellow flowered dress? Paisley silk shawl? Sexy black pants? Jeans and a white T-shirt? Red dress with a swishy skirt? Fall velvety blazer? What do these items have in common?

Finally, never forget that the most essential fashion accessories, the ones no woman can do without, come from within. A generous heart, a spontaneous smile, and

Sarah Ban Breathnach

eyes that sparkle with delight can be part of any woman's signature look once she awakens to her authentic beauty.

Let's go back to a time when many of us not only felt wonderful but knew we were. We do this exercise in my workshops, but you can do it with a friend. Each of you find a picture of yourself from when you were ten years old. Study one another's photos and tell each other what you see. A beautiful girl with open eyes, a warm smile, a spirit of adventure? Look at your friend's picture and at your own. Look lovingly and compassionately at those girls. Write down what you see when you look at her photo, and at your own:

Her Photo   Your Photo

*Our deepest wishes
are whispers of our
authentic selves.
We must learn
to respect them.
We must learn
to listen.*

SIMPLE ABUNDANCE
JANUARY 29

What usually happens in the workshops is that we are more generous with, we see more deeply into, the photograph of another. Now you must learn to try to bring the same kind of surprise and delight and openness to your own picture.

Look at the picture as if it were of your own child; when we look at our own children, we love them without reservation. Even when we're mad at them, we still love them unconditionally. And that's the place we're trying to get to when we think of ourselves.

How does your picture make you feel? Do you want to put your arms around this girl, comfort her, encourage her, love her?

Try to encapsulate in a few sentences who this girl was, and what woman she has become. What does she love, what has been her journey?

Now I'd like you to say aloud this poem by Maya Angelou:

Phenomenal Woman

Pretty women wonder where my secret lies.
I'm not cute or built to suit a fashion model's size
But when I start to tell them,
They think I'm telling lies.
I say,
It's in the reach of my arms,
The span of my hips,
The stride of my step,
The curl of my lips.
I'm a woman
Phenomenally.
Phenomenal woman,
That's me.

I walk into a room
Just as cool as you please,
And to a man,
The fellows stand or
Fall down on their knees.
Then they swarm around me,
A hive of honey bees.
I say,
It's the fire in my eyes,
And the flash of my teeth,
The swing in my waist,
And the joy in my feet.
I'm a woman
Phenomenally.
Phenomenal woman,
That's me.

Men themselves have wondered
What they see in me.
They try so much.
But they can't touch
My inner mystery.
When I try to show them,
They say they still can't see.
I say,
It's in the arch of my back,
The sun of my smile,
the ride of my breasts,
The grace of my style.
I'm a woman

Phenomenally.
Phenomenal woman,
That's me.

Now you understand
Just why my head's not bowed.
I don't shout or jump about
Or have to talk real loud.
When you see me passing,
It ought to make you proud.
I say,
It's in the click of my heels,
The bend of my hair,
The palm of my hand,
The need for my care.
'Cause I'm a woman
Phenomenally.
Phenomenal woman,
That's me.

Isn't this poem glorious? How does that make you feel? Talk about a howl for joy. Guess what? You are phenomenal, and that's what you're going to discover, that's what you are going to realize: just how phenomenal you really are.

Invite a friend to join you in the next exercise as well. Just look into one another's faces deeply. Each of you really look at the other, as though seeing one another for the first time.

Be silent as you do the exercise. (And if you don't

have a friend handy right now, just look into a mirror.) This should be a sacred exercise. Look at your partner, gaze at her. Study her with your eyes, and then go deeper. Allow your heart to guide your vision, and see her with all the openness of your heart and soul.

Rumi, the Sufi poet, said a very powerful prayer, which is, "Oh Divine One, please enlarge my heart so that I might receive thy love." And that is what I'm asking you to be open to doing now; asking Spirit to enlarge your heart so that you will have space for more love—not for others, but for yourself.

Now find and list five things about your partner that are absolutely extraordinary and beautiful, and phenomenal:

So what did you list? Beautiful soft hair? Sparkling, expressive eyes? A warm smile? An accepting look? A dimple? Freckles? Graceful hand? Serene composure? Vitality? Strong cheekbones? A sense of humor? Radiant smile? And what did your partner list about you?

Phenomenal Woman, I want you to write these things in your Self-Gratitude Journal, so that the next time you look at yourself in the mirror you can see the beauty that your partner discerned there today. Look at yourself with the same appreciation, wonderment, and admiration.

A personal prompt that I love involves an oil painting. If you could put yourself into any picture, what picture would it be?

When I went on this search, I knew her as soon as I saw her—she is "Madam X," in an 1884 painting by John Singer Sargent. The painting was completely scandalous when it was completed. Madam X's dress was too low. She was too strong. She was too bold—"brazen" was the word that was used. She was too arrogant. She was too, too, too. She was too much for the male critics to take in 1884. She was too much because she was a Phenomenal Woman and was very proud. In the picture she is looking away from the viewer's gaze because she is rejecting the confines of society's definitions of right and wrong. She is looking for the landscape that is larger than the one that she can see.

I encourage you to make a creative excursion to an exhibition, or to the library. From the collections of paintings you see on museum walls or in books, look for something that calls to you. You can get a color copy of it if it's in a book, or if it's in a museum you can often buy a print or postcard. Put it in your Illustrated Discovery Journal. Use it to meditate on.

If you have been dressing so that you will fade into the woodwork, because you wouldn't be able to cope with all the admiration, how would you really like to look? How could you dress yourself radiantly so that everyone who sees you would say "Whew!"? As Mae West reminds us, "I'd rather get looked over than overlooked." So would I. Imagine handling all that attention with ease. What would you wear?

Reconsider Your Reflection

Get rid of the tendency
to judge yourself
above, below, or
equal to others.

ABHIRUPA-NANDA

It's time for you to discover who's really the fairest of them all when you gaze into your mirror. Tonight, or sometime soon when you have a peace-

There's a lot that's luscious about you, although you're probably bound to disagree. Why do you play down all your assets and call attention to your deficits? We've got to change that.

SOMETHING MORE
"THE BOOK OF LOVE"

ful hour to yourself and are neither harried nor hurried—perhaps after a relaxing bath—try this: Look at yourself in a full-length mirror, and clear away any of the familiar critical thoughts that crowd your mind. Take in your appearance from head to toe slowly and with appreciation. Now compliment yourself. Find ten things you love about your face or body—yes, you can do it.

Be specific. I love the color of my eyes. I love my long eyelashes. I love the way my mouth looks when I smile. I love how my hair curls behind my ear. I love my straight shoulders. I love my long, slender neck. I love my cleavage. I love my toes. Say your compliments out loud using nurturing, praising words, and write them all down.

Now keep going and praise your fabulous personality. Find ten things, both big and small, that you admire in yourself: I am a loving mother, a hard worker, a patient teacher, good seamstress, a compassionate friend, a talented cook. Feel proud of yourself—and it will show in the expression on your face and the way you hold your body.

Repeat these empowering words aloud every morning and every night as you look in the mirror. Take your time. Believe what you are saying. It's all true.

An exercise I used to help me learn to become comfortable in my own skin was to not wear clothes when I was by myself in my bedroom. I started by sleeping in the nude, then lingered without dressing after a shower. As I spent more time actually aware of my body, I started appreciating all the amazing things she does for me every day.

Pay attention to the way your body moves throughout the day, from the moment you swing your legs out of bed in the morning until you lie back down at night. If your body allows you to swim, to dance, to sit, to stand, to walk down the street, to hug a friend, to climb a hill, to ride a bike, shouldn't you acknowledge these enormous feats? Your body allows you to make love, give birth, and nourish a child. It takes you everywhere you want to go. Your body exists to work for you—not against you. Don't you want to stop working against her?

Catch yourself when you start thinking that you would be more happy or successful or intelligent if only you could be thinner or prettier. As you interact with the people you love, remind yourself what it is that you admire about them: their generosity, their warmth, their sense of humor, their ease with conversation. Not their appearance. Be aware that they are looking at you in the same way, and accept every compliment graciously.

Now that you've discovered the attractive, talented woman that you are, appreciate her every day. When you look in the mirror, talk to yourself in words you deserve to hear. Reframe how you describe yourself. Your legs are powerful; your arms are strong; your stomach is soft and cuddly; your hips are womanly.

Today, and every day, take as your personal mantra, "I am what I am and what I am is wonderful."

For you are a Phenomenal Woman.

The Other Woman

People are prone to build a statue of the kind of person that it pleases them to be. And few people want to be forced to ask themselves, "What if there is no me like my statue?"

ZORA NEALE HURSTON

Women separate into two distinct groups when they hear the phrase "the other woman." Whether we hear about her via gossip around the water cooler, over a cup of coffee with a friend, or in the national news, we either fear or understand her. In either case, we feel strongly one way or the other because more than just our marriages are threatened by infidelity.

If we identify with "the other woman" more often than not, it's because we are her, or have been her at some point during our lives. There are many ways to be seen as "the other woman" besides losing your way in love's guaranteed labyrinth of loss—an affair with a married man. Perhaps you lured away your college roommate's boyfriend fifteen years ago, or regularly flirt with a coworker's husband at social gatherings. And as strange as this seems, many a mistress would describe her lover's wife as the other woman, especially on weekends and holidays.

The power we surrender to this feminine figment of fear is enormous. If she poaches our man, not only does she steal our life, our security, and our identities, she devalues our self-worth. That's why her specter is particularly frightening during those times when we're feeling lost and insecure, exhausted and out of shape; when we suspect in the wee small hours of the morning that our marriage continues to exist not because of shared dreams and mutual passions but because there is a mortgage to pay, kids to pick up after school, and shared friends. Does this sound at all familiar? A dear friend admitted it took her years before she realized that her jealousy over the time her husband spent with his female coworkers was directly proportional to the highs and lows she experienced on the scale each morning.

"The other woman" scares us at these moments because she is everything we are not. She is more beautiful, more sexy, more intelligent, more savvy than you are. She has the assured presence to pull off the fabulous evening dress you've been lusting after in the store window for months but haven't had the confidence to even try on. She has the aplomb and verve to tell an artful joke at a cocktail party that sets the whole room laughing. She has the spontaneity and freedom to plan a weekend getaway on a Thursday night. She's a more sophisticated cook than you, has skinnier thighs, and is no doubt more uninhibited in bed. She lights up a room and draws every man's—your man's—eyes to her. Go ahead, list all the traits of your ultimate other woman.

Now step back a second. Who exactly are you describing here?

"The other woman"'s comeliness is usually very specific. Could it be tailored to what we feel are our own shortcomings and flaws? Take another close look at your list. Does this sound like anyone your husband even knows? Who, then, have you described? And why is "the other woman" most threatening when you're unhappy with yourself? What if that's because your unseen rival is really you?

As hard as this truth is to process, I have learned that you are always "the other woman" in your own intimate relationships, because "the other woman" is your Authentic Self.

Your Authentic Self is the sexy, beautiful, creative, confident, accomplished, amazing siren you have forgotten about, ignored, buried alive. It is not a coincidence that you become most obsessed with the possibility of another woman during the times when you feel completely isolated and estranged from your own soul. She is the manifestation of your fears and denial in the flesh.

The truth is, when we deny who we are, when we deny who and what we love, when we disown our authenticity, we are unfaithful to ourselves. (Forget worrying about your husband cheating on you.) You've been cheating on yourself. And if you've been unfaithful to yourself, what's to stop anyone else from doing the same thing? As Erica Jong asks, "In any triangle, who is the betrayer, who is the unseen rival and who is the humiliated lover?

Oneself, oneself, and no one but oneself."

Today, pick up a mirror and look in it until you see Spirit's truth reflected back. You are a woman of great style and enormous substance. Did you know that? You are a woman of beauty, intelligence, vision, warmth, power, influence, strength, wit, generosity, compassion, and soul. And if you don't see this, you've been looking for your worth in all the wrong faces, and I don't care who you live with.

SOMETHING MORE
"SEEING IS
BELIEVING"

The Scarlet Letter

The knives of jealousy are honed on details.

Ruth Rendell

Jealousy and envy are adulterous sins against your authenticity. Comparing ourselves with other women hurts us in profound ways. It undermines our confidence and shuts down our flow of creative energy. It short-circuits our access to spiritual electricity and depletes our self-esteem. It sucks the life force from the marrow of our souls.

Comparisons are irresistible, insidious, odious, and very often our self-torture of choice. But it's easier to recover from physical abuse than self-inflicted psychic brutality.

Sometimes "the other woman" haunting our lives isn't a romantic rival. She can be your accomplished, cellulite-free friend, another account executive, a mother in the PTA. Whoever she is, she's the devil's daughter because you insist on measuring your life, success, bank account, marriage, or self-worth against hers.

Usually it's only one woman whose bounteous blessings push our buttons of raging insecurity; we really don't care if most of the world has more than we have, we only care that "she" has and we have not. Sometimes the subject of our hostility is not even personally known to us, though the glorious good life she leads in print is. Secretly we stalk the newspapers and magazines accumulating evidence of *her* good fortune instead of using our time, creative energy, and emotion to create our own.

Even when we've done something wonderful that we should enjoy gloating about, we deny ourselves the pleasure of recognition. Women are rarely comfortable basking in the glow of accomplishment. Instead, we feel the need to downplay our achievements. We shrug off personal triumphs as if they were flukes, then wonder why we feel so unfulfilled.

If we trace this unnurturing behavior back to its source, many of us will find ourselves standing quietly, waiting patiently for the parental approval that never came. Decades later, because we have been conditioned to believe that nothing we do is ever good enough, we continue this destructive cycle of withholding approval from ourselves.

I struggled with this lesson most of my life. Since I hadn't received recognition or approval from my parents and certainly didn't give it to myself, the only possible source was the outside world. Surely the world would notice, in a meaningful way, my next project.

But why should it when I didn't? I experienced this awakening one day when I was rewriting my résumé for a new venture. As I listed my accomplishments I wondered, "Who is this woman?" because if detectives had arrived at my door to search for her, they wouldn't have found a shred of physical evidence.

So I started excavating for clues, rescuing proof that I'd scaled mountains when all I gave myself credit for was rolling out of bed. And there, literally "buried" in the basement, were cardboard boxes full of treasures. As I unearthed myself I was as thrilled, I imagine, as the famous Egyptologist Howard Carter when he found the tomb of the Egyptian boy-king Tutankhamen.

After I relived my days of triumph, I took some of my favorite memorabilia—book covers, the announcement of my newspaper column—to the framers. When I hung them up in the living room it was exhilarating. Then I began to congratulate myself out loud for the jobs well done. Now I ransom moments of achievement from personal amnesia by giving them physical presence.

How can you do this as well? What were some of your moments of glory? How can you celebrate them?

Only you can confer the recognition that will make you feel fulfilled because only you know what you truly need.

Chapter 4 — Moodlings

Phenomenal Woman

1. It's amazing. When you feel good on the inside, it shows on the outside. This week, make an effort to stand a little straighter, or to smile more often. Record the reactions you get. How does this make you feel?

2. Here is an exercise to try with your Illustrated Discovery Journal: Think back through your life to the times you felt most attractive, sexiest, most confident. Can you picture what you were wearing at the time? Go through your photo albums, yearbooks, and scrapbooks and see if there is physical evidence. Between these two resources, can you establish any patterns—do you "smile" more in outfits that are tight-fitting or loose and flowy, bright solid colors or small subtle prints, shiny material or matte black? Record your findings in your Illustrated Discovery Journal or below.

3. This month, put the word "indulgence" back into your active vocabulary by:

    Bathing by candlelight, with bubbles that smell of your favorite flowers or the most invigorating mint.

    Taking a few extra minutes to massage your scalp as you shampoo.

Scrubbing your feet smooth with a pumice stone; and after you pat yourself dry, caress yourself with lotion.

Reclining with cool cucumber slices over your eyes, or giving yourself a soothing face mask. Write down on an index card the new routine you're going to do every evening, including a beauty treatment, until this self-nurturing ritual becomes as habitual as brushing your teeth.

Experience the miracle of your body. You know that exercise is good for you, but forget about that for now. Instead, just focus on how good it feels to pump your arms as you walk briskly, to kick your legs as you swim, to shake your hips as you dance, to breathe deeply, to think calmly. Every few days, do something that makes you break out in a sweat, from jumping rope to a brisk walk around your neighborhood. See if simply *moving* doesn't make you feel more energetic, make you sleep better, make you like your body even more. See if you don't want to keep on moving. So do it. (Now you can remember that exercise is good for you too.)

Let yourself shine. Accepting your appearance unconditionally does not mean giving up makeup or not coloring your hair. On the contrary, it may give you the motivation to express yourself in ways you've never dared to—but always dreamed of. Stop hiding behind clothes and makeup that let you blend in rather than stand out. If you love your full lips, show them off with the perfect shade of lipstick. If you love fabulous hats, long silk scarves, high heels, bangle bracelets, wear them. Is there something you've been dying to try—rhinestone hair clips, a batik sarong skirt, flamboyant earrings? What is it? Try it this week.

Write Your Way into Wholeness

Get Out of Your Own Way

Regrets are as personal as fingerprints.

Margaret Culkin Banning

Chapter 5

Courage

Luck is not chance—
It's Toil—
Fortune's expensive smile
Is earned.

Emily Dickinson

Do you secretly believe that the women who have whatever it is that you don't and desperately want—naturally curly hair, a husband who cleans the kitchen, a perfect body, or a comma in the checking account balance—were just born lucky?

Growing up I loved the promise of good fortune encompassed in the magical phrase "the luck of the Irish." Since my birthright virtually guaranteed success, there wasn't much doubt in my mind that I would lead a charmed life. Then one night I overheard my parents talking about some ancient "family curse" that ensured that no matter how much success any of us had, we would always end up as failures. To prove their point they reeled off a litany of misery suffered by a list of relations going back four generations that sent shudders up my adolescent spine.

The next week my boyfriend broke up with me three days before the prom. When I didn't get into my first-choice college and lost my job after moving into my first apartment, I wondered if I was a marked woman.

Have you ever felt like that? Maybe your family

91

Sarah Ban Breathnach

Suspend disbelief.
Experiment with a
loving, supportive
Universe that embraces
even skeptics. . . . Be
willing to believe that a
companion Spirit is
leading you every step
of the way, and knows
the next step.

SIMPLE ABUNDANCE
JANUARY 21

doesn't have an official curse, but do you have your own superstitions? What about good-luck charms? Perhaps you stroke the tiny emerald chip on your grandmother's locket for good luck, hold on to a grubby-looking rabbit's foot or wear an angel pin. It's all pretty much the same thing. But whether we monitor the movement of the planets, lunge for the wishbone, or knock on wood in the middle of conversation—and I've done all three—any superstition is only as powerful as we allow it to become.

I know a woman who swears that if she eats at a particular Japanese restaurant before a new client presentation, she'll land the big account. It's happened three times in a row. Unfortunately, the restaurant recently went out of business and she's terrified that this will have an effect on her job. Another woman I know, who married for the first time at forty, always dreamed of being a mother. Despite the anguish of three pregnancies that never came to term and being turned down twice by adoption agencies because she and her husband were "too old," she refused to relinquish her dream. This inner knowing opened her heart to a different possibility. She now has a beautiful four-year-old daughter, adopted from China. The first woman put herself at the mercy of whim and outward circumstance. The second woman turned inward, and the depth of her faith allowed her to push past limitation.

The sad truth is that it took me many years of my life to realize that as long as I believed I was unlucky, life would provide me with all the proof I needed to confirm my fears. Then during my twenties I was invited to an unusual potluck supper that came with a warning: "Just remember, dinner will only be as good as the offering you bring." At the time, most of us could barely boil an egg, but we all rose to the challenge. It was one of the most memorable meals I've ever enjoyed because each guest's dish was more scrumptious than the next. As one woman put it, what she lacked in culinary talent she made up for with enthusiasm.

After that I decided to think about life not as a game of chance but as a potluck supper. The success of the meal would depend on how much time, creative energy, love, and emotion I could expend on the recipe and what raw ingredients were in the cupboard. If I wasn't born lucky, I would compensate for it with my own brand of enthusiasm; I'd throw in a pinch of pluck, perseverance, and prayer. And you know a little spice goes a long way.

After *Simple Abundance* (which was my third book) became a surprise best-seller, my brother called to congratulate me for "breaking" the family curse. There's no question in my mind that my stubborn faith enabled me to keep going despite thirty rejections. But perhaps more than two decades of writing and experience gleaned from all my "unlucky" incidents had something to do with my success. Nothing dies harder than a limiting illusion, whether it's a charm, a curse, or conventional wisdom.

Now I laugh when strangers describe me as Lady Luck, though I don't disagree with them. But isn't it fascinating that the harder you work, the more risks you take, and the more "thanks" you send up to Heaven, the luckier you seem to get? I agree with Emily Dickinson: fortune's smile is earned.

Taking Risks

If you risk nothing, then you risk everything.

GEENA DAVIS

Psychologist Susan Jeffers suggests that we "take a risk a day—one small or bold stroke that makes you feel great once you have done it." Today, take a real risk that can change your life: start thinking of yourself as an artist and your life as a work-in-progress. Works-in-progress are never perfect, but changes can be made to the rough draft during rewrites. Art evolves. So does life. The beautiful, authentic life you are creating for yourself and those you love is your art. What risks would you love to have the nerve to take, even very small ones? List three:

Each of us is an artist. An artist is merely someone with good listening skills who accesses the creative energy of the Universe to bring forth something on the physical plane that wasn't here before.

So it is with creating an authentic life. With every choice, every day, you are creating a unique work of art, something that only you can do. Don't try to remake yourself into something you're not, just try making the best of what God has made. Making the best of ourselves is the reason we were born, but it requires patience and perseverance. For many of us it also requires prayer.

Each time you experience the new, you become receptive to inspiration. Each time you try something different, you let the Universe know you are listening.

We fear the unknown. We fear failure. But even more, we are afraid of succeeding, of becoming our authentic selves and facing the changes *that* will bring. We may not be happy with the way we're living now, but at least it's familiar. Perhaps most of all we fear isolation. Isolation from our family, our spouse, our friends, job, our community. This may be the most difficult challenge of all. And yet we don't become authentic by playing small, by hiding (or denying) our best selves, refusing to stand out.

When you take risks, expect to have hope rekindled. Expect your prayers to be answered in wondrous ways. Heaven applauds your courage. So should you.

Life's Currency

If you're never scared or embarrassed or hurt,
it means you never take any chances.

JULIA SOREL

In an interview in the *New York Times* about ten years ago, Oprah Winfrey, who is a very spiritual woman, said, "I don't think that the expression that we're not given more than we can handle refers to just the tragedies in our lives. If you can't handle the good stuff, if you can't handle money, or a good relationship, or success, you're not going to get it. It will only be given to you when you can handle it."

When I read this I thought, whoa—the good things as well as the bad? Almost immediately there was a deep inner shift in my reality and I "got it." I don't think I would have been able to write *Simple Abundance* without the awareness that we have to push past our comfort zone to handle the good as well as the bad in life.

Once we were going to set the world on fire. But over the years we've buried many a precious dream. It's no wonder that we'll need courage to retrace our steps. But "courage is the price that Life extracts for granting peace," the pilot Amelia Earhart reminds us.

Courage is the currency with which we pay for life. It requires enormous courage to look truth straight in the eye and accept it as your reality, to bless a situation because there's a hidden gift in it for you.

We can stop waiting for life to become perfect and start working with what we've got to make it as satisfying as we can. We can accept, bless, give thanks, and get going.

SIMPLE ABUNDANCE
JANUARY 25

96

A friend of mine knew the great undersea explorer Jacques-Yves Cousteau. Once, when Cousteau was about to address the United Nations, he gave my friend a preview of what he was going to tell the Assembly—that it takes enormous courage to clean up the environment, to stop polluting the seas, but that *we always pay for lack of courage.* I love that thought, which sometimes gives me the courage to act when a task is difficult.

It takes great love and courage to excavate buried dreams. We cannot change our past choices now, but we can build on them, we can redirect them. We can take them into consideration as we ponder new choices.

Perhaps a long-buried dream still calls to you from a road you chose not to take. If so, stop telling yourself that it's too late. The delay of our dreams does not mean that they have been denied. Perhaps now you have the wisdom to make alterations in your dream so that it can come true. Perhaps you are brave enough to accept the pleasure and commitment it could bring.

The Courage to Have No Regrets

Never regret. If it's good, it's wonderful.
If it's bad, it's experience.

VICTORIA HOLT

Every morning when I awake, I ask my soul this question: "If I die tonight, what would I regret not having done today?" Do I need to say, "I love you"? "I forgive you"? "I'm sorry"? If I do, it's the first telephone call I make.

Ask your soul the same question. What things would you regret not doing today? We can't change past transgressions, except to let them go. We can, however, do something now so that we'll have little need in the future to think, "I should have . . ."

What brave action can you take in the present so that you won't have regrets in the future? What are some things that you can do now so that someday you won't say, "If only . . ."? Is there one small action you can take to nurture your new dreams toward fruition? If there is, put it at the top of your to-do list:

Ask yourself, "If I should be blessed with tomorrow, is there a choice that I *can* make, *need* to make, or *want* to make that could enhance the quality of my life? Is there one I'm postponing because it's difficult or painful? If I ignore it, will it be the regret I take with me?" If there is a chance it will, then make room in your heart and your schedule to think about it, and maybe even act on it.

Life is a work-in-progress because life is art, the highest art. Your Authentic Self is the voice of your wisdom, the voice of passion. She speaks the dialect of desire. It is your rational self that speaks common sense. This is the voice that says, "Let's be reasonable, let's rethink this."

That is not your Authentic Self. Your Authentic Self says, "I know you're a little nervous about doing this and yes, it means we're going to have to push past your comfort zone just a bit, but you'll feel great when we get to the other side." And that will happen in choices that you make. Maybe it's as simple as a fabulous outfit you're working up the courage to wear, or a place you're scared to go, a difficult conversation you'd like to start. The comfort zone for all of us is that well-padded perimeter of the familiar. Think of your limitations as a padded box. We're very comfortable in there, but in order for us to get to the other side, where our Authentic Self is waiting to take us, we have to push.

Your Authentic Self is your rational self's worst nightmare. Because when your Authentic Self starts to make her presence known, and helps you make your new courageous choice, the old ways are no longer your standard operating procedure. Things are going to change. But Ms. Rational likes it just the way it is, thank you very much. "It's taken me your entire life to orchestrate things this way and I don't want any changes," says the ego.

That's where we start to get conflict against pushing past the comfort zone, because the rational self brings out the big guns of fear and intimidation. We know what fear is—we feel it when our hands are shaking, we feel it in our stomachs, when we can't sleep, when we're so scared we think we're going to cry, when we're so tight we tremble. Fear usually manifests itself in a physical form. Fear is not subtle, but intimidation is.

Any actor or actress will tell you that they feel fear before they go onstage—that's stage fright. But as they push past this, the anxiety transforms into creativity. Think of anxiety as the overture to the "zone," that amazing current of spiritual electricity.

But intimidation knows all the right buttons to press for each of us. So one minute she'll say, "I'm the only one who realizes how difficult your life is right now. I am the one who knows how much you have to do, and I know that you're too tired to sit down and write that new résumé. C'mon, give yourself a break."

Or she says, "Look, it was a foolish idea to begin with. Look at you, you're too old. You don't have the money. You don't have the support system. What if you fail? You probably will fail, because someone who tries something like this is crazy."

Intimidation always sounds reasonable, she always makes sense. Your ego is terrified you'll get in touch with your Authentic Self, because when you do she's out of a job as your control freak.

But believe me, as soon as you break out beyond that comfort zone you will feel truly alive. Strangely enough, the smallest thing can do it. A conversation, a new and different haircut, a smile at a stranger.

What is this search for authenticity? It's searching for the Real, for what means the most to you on this earth, what you really want to do, what you really want to say, how you truly want to express yourself, artistically, creatively, and spiritually. Whether it's a garden or a meal, whatever it is. Authenticity is what makes you happy.

Begin to listen for the whisper of your Authentic Self telling you which way to go. The psychologist Carl Rogers said that when people begin to heal and become more psychologically healthy, often they don't yet know what it is they really want. But they *do* know what they want to move away from, and they begin eliminating those things from their lives.

Don't you want to start making happiness a habit right now? Let's stop thinking that things outside our control will bring us happiness. The magic seeds of contentment are planted deep within us. Happiness that the world cannot take away only flourishes in the secret garden of our souls. Happiness is a *living* emotion. Today you may not be familiar with the "happiness habit." But like any new behavior, happiness can be learned.

Ask yourself: "What is it I truly need to make me happy?" It is only after we acknowledge our inner needs that we can harness the creative energy necessary to manifest them in our lives. What do you need? Health, enough money to get by, friends, work, home, love, learning, curiosity, meaning? List what you require:

Both authenticity and adventure require a point of departure, the willingness to shed what's safe and predictable in order to embrace the new— people, places, predicaments, pleasures, and passions. Your new, authentic life.

SOMETHING MORE
"THE SACRED
ADVENTURE"

Dress Rehearsals

*It is best . . . to act with confidence no
matter how little right you have to it.*

LILLIAN HELLMAN

It seems surprising that so much courage should
be needed just to live the destinies that we are
yearning to fulfill. The lives for which we were born.

One workshop member, a shy single woman, described how one day she was in a strange city, waiting to
meet a man she didn't know. She was doing some business with his company, and they were to get together at
the hotel bar at 5:30 P.M. When she arrived in the bar she
looked around, spoke to a few people and asked if they
were Mr. X, but not one said yes. So she sat down at a
table, smiling and at ease, and as people came in she
asked if they were Mr. X. Finally Mr. X arrived, and they
had their drink and conversation. But she couldn't help
realizing afterward how comfortable she had felt alone
in that bar *because she felt entitled to be there.*

Her story led me to conduct an exercise.

Many of us behave in a relaxed and open manner
when we feel "entitled" to be somewhere, when we feel
comfortable in ourselves. In one workshop, we under-
took some "dress rehearsals." There were certain things
the women wanted to do but were afraid to try.

Sometimes if we can feel as though an event is practice, as though it doesn't really count, we can enjoy it, go with the flow, and let go of expectations.

We broke into small groups. One woman who wanted to stand up to a colleague at work "role-played" the scene with her partner, trying out the things she wanted to say to him. The other woman, acting as the colleague, responded spontaneously. Afterward the woman doing the role-playing felt more confident (actually they both did!).

Another woman pretended to be an interviewer, while a workshop member nervous about going back to work was the interviewee. They ran through some questions ("What do you think qualifies you for this job?" "Why do you want this job?" "Why did you leave your last job?" "Haven't you been out of touch with this field for a long time?"). As we watched them, it was obvious that the women became more comfortable as they continued to role-play.

I used to yearn to shop in an exclusive store on Madison Avenue in New York. But since I was coming from lack, I could never find enough courage to cross its threshold. What would happen if I really fell in love with a $5,000 gown? So I denied myself the pleasure of even browsing anywhere more upscale than Sears or Kmart.

But if you stand on Madison Avenue and look at the people going in to Armani, or Valentino, you can't tell which ones are rich. Sometimes they are the worst-dressed people imaginable. F. Scott Fitzgerald declared that the rich "are different from you and me." What was he talking about? Attitude. The very rich "possess and enjoy early . . . ," and one of the things they possess is the feeling of entitlement. Belonging anywhere they want to be.

Wealth is as much a state of mind as it is money in the bank. Let me give you an example. You go up to the ATM and it swallows your card. Now, most people who live from paycheck to paycheck will automatically assume they've mismanaged their checkbook and are overdrawn. It feels terrible and irresponsible. Financial shame is hard to shake, even when you know that it's the machine that's having the breakdown, not you. A person who knows there's plenty of money in the account, who probably doesn't even have to worry about balancing her checkbook, will react in this way: "Damn, that's an inconvenience." Do you see the difference?

There's so much in life that we think we can't do. But if you did have an extra $5,000 to spend, I'm willing to bet you wouldn't want to spend it on the first item with that price tag. Next time, instead of declaring to the Universe, "I can't afford this," have the courage to say, "I can afford anything I want. I simply choose not to spend my money this way right now." Life takes you at your word.

When a friend of mine turned forty she bought herself a fur coat, which depleted her disposable cash dramatically. But she looked and felt glorious in her new adornment and radiated a sense of well-being. One day she was browsing in an upscale haunt in her new coat and she realized that the salespeople were rushing up to help her. And she thought, "Last month, when I had money to spend, you ignored me. Now that I have no money to spend, you pay attention." Go figure.

Unfortunately, it's true that our outside packaging counts for far more than it really should. Remember Julia Roberts's shopping expedition in the film *Pretty Woman*? "The tragedy of our time is that we are . . . so appearance besotted," the writer Jessamyn West confesses. Often, when we don't live up to the world's expectations of how we should look or behave, we fall victim to a vicious cycle of self-loathing and denial that can be difficult to escape from unscathed. But once we realize our habitual thought patterns, we can choose when and where we belong.

There is a wonderful, very funny scene in Robert Hellenga's novel *The Fall of a Sparrow* in which a father prepares his daughter for a job interview. Insisting that she get dressed up, he conducts the practice interview in straight-backed dining room chairs. When she flounders around, he tells her, "You have to remember that most people will want to help you if you get them in the right frame of mind. If they think they're on your side, or you're on their side." You can practice these "get them on your side" exercises at home. Do them with your husband, a neighbor, or a friend. Have your partner play the person who is to interview you for a new position.

The aim is for you to be able to go anywhere and feel open, relaxed, entitled to be there and comfortable in your own skin. This is what authenticity feels like.

If you'd like to have a big dinner party at home, try

Regret is the only wound from which the soul never recovers.

SOMETHING MORE
"THE MORTAL
WOUND"

out your menu with a few "safe" family members and friends before you prepare it for a more formal gathering. Even on your practice run, set up the dining room table, use place cards.

Wear your fancy dress to be sure there are no tags hanging from it, that the fit is good. Make sure it's comfortable, that there are no split seams, missing buttons, no stains. Walk around, sit down. All of us, I believe, have a fear of being exposed as an impostor, a fraud. But give yourself permission to be who you are, anyplace in the world.

If It Feels Scary, You're Making Progress

Fear is a sign—usually a sign that I'm doing something right.

ERICA JONG

Right now, list five things that you would love to do but that seem beyond your comfort zone. Things you feel exhilarated about but frightened to try. What new experiences are these? Would you like to take acting lessons? Become more spontaneous, tearing down the emotional wall of control you've built around yourself? Wear something daring, make a speech, become chairman of an organization? Put an ad in the singles section of a magazine, or answer one? Go on a tour of Turkey by yourself? Write an article? Go to Victoria's Secret and buy sexy red lacy underwear?

What's on your list?

How about a dress rehearsal? Who feels safe enough for you to try them with?

Act as if you're self-confident, and the world will take you as such. You can always borrow a self-confident attitude from your Authentic Self. She knows how terrific you are and can give you that little boost, which is all you really need. Remember that your subconscious mind can't distinguish between what is real and what is imaginary—which is why creative visualization works. If we act as if we are confident, we become so.

Bring the power back to yourself. Don't worry about "What isn't he going to like about me?" Instead wonder, "Am I going to like him? Is this job right for me? Is this neighborhood right for me and my family?" Shift your concern from other people's opinions to your own and the balance of power, the center of gravity, returns to you. You'll be self-centered in a healthy way.

There are moments today when I get very frightened about something that's asked of me, and I'll say, "I can't do that." "I don't know how to do this." "I am so tired of flying by the seat of my pants." That's the small me, the child, who's talking. And then my Authentic Self, who is the adult me, will say, "That's okay. I know how to do this. Just come along with me." When I do, I'm always delighted at the result.

Really, that's what's so wonderful about risk. We don't have to get it right the first time. That is what experimentation is—playful investigation. Think of risk as a game. If you watch children play, you'll notice how much they improvise. We can do that too. They test, repeat, try again. There is a spontaneity about experimentation, and children don't see it as failure.

I was sitting at breakfast one day with several men, and they were talking about wanting to establish in the South a kind of visionary center like the Omega Institute in Rhinebeck, New York. They'd wanted to do this for years but had never been able to get things together. They didn't have the land, they didn't have the money, they didn't have this, they didn't have that.

So I recommended they start searching for their site as if their center was ready to be built.

They just looked at me in astonishment. In that moment I understood why their center is still a figment of their imaginations.

If you can dream it, it can be done. What you're really doing when you take the first step is saying to the Universe, "I am very serious about this plan." And that is all the Universe is waiting to hear from you.

One woman in a workshop spoke of how she used to feel as if she was drifting, that she was without power. She felt that power was outside herself, generated from external sources like the wind. She felt buffeted. She decided that to find a way out of this, she would take just one action, one single assertion of herself, each day. She now wisely asks herself each day, "What can I do today to become courageous in a tangible way?" In doing that, she has truly learned that self-esteem grows when we are taking action on our own behalf.

Daunting Courage

You must do the thing you think you cannot do.

ELEANOR ROOSEVELT

Setting boundaries requires courage. The word *courage* comes from the French word for the heart, *coeur.*

Many women of a certain age today are coping with the fact that just as their children have left home and they themselves are launched in work or volunteer programs that they love, their husbands are retiring and coming back home.

In some cases, after a woman has been called on to do many things alone because her husband was constantly on business trips or working long hours, this means a big adjustment. Now her husband is home all the time, and her routines and sense of personal autonomy are thrown off. She hasn't the "heart" to hurt his feelings, so she buries hers. One woman in a workshop described how her husband now wants to come with her every time she goes somewhere, even to the grocery store.

A friend of mine who just remarried went from being with a man who didn't want anything to do with her to being married to a man who worships the ground she walks on and doesn't want her out of his sight. While she relishes being adored like this, she is feeling a bit stifled. So she has begun to help her new husband rediscover the things he liked to do on his own. On Mondays, Wednesdays, and Fridays she gets her two hours; on Thursdays they do something together.

When you encounter your Authentic Self, when your passion comes alive again, you don't have to leave your job, your marriage, your relationship—unless those are the right choices for you. You learn to have the courage to integrate yourself, whole, fully alive, with the world around you. And you have the courage to do that because you learn slowly and gently how to *set boundaries* on how much you will let other people tell you what to do and define you. You will learn how to say enough is enough, how to take time for yourself.

In her fascinating book *The Heroine's Journey,*

Maureen Murdock tells us, "The single greatest challenge for most women is to achieve balance among relationships, work, and time alone. *Women have to be willing to find the courage to set limits and say no* [emphasis in original]."

Be patient. Don't expect too much too soon, especially when rearranging your schedule means dealing with your family's expectations of what you're supposed to do and when you're supposed to do it.

But be firm as well. In *Something More* I told the story of a pediatric surgical nurse who married her high school sweetheart, had five children, and was beautifully provided for by her husband. However, when her children were grown and she wanted to go back to nursing, her husband objected. It can be a very delicate situation when our authentic dreams interfere with other people's plans and lifestyles. Joanne stifled her passion to return to work, but she couldn't see that her biggest risk was in settling, in playing it safe. She has changed, and she wants to preserve her marriage. But can her marriage be flexible enough to encompass her growth?

When we lose touch with our true natures, we are unable to create boundaries that protect, nurture, and sustain our self-worth. We forget that we're first-rate women and try to play down to the rest of the world so that we'll be accepted. But if you want to be admired, adored, and loved, you're going to have to hold out.

So your relationships are going to change. But they are going to change in positive and empowering ways.

You're going to be able to say, "This is precious to me. I cherish this and I want to keep it sacred and that is my path."

One workshop participant talked about her relationship with her demanding mother-in-law, with whom she has been struggling for years. The mother-in-law keeps telling this woman she is selfish. "If I listened to everything she said about selfishness and played it out to the end, she would take everything good in my life that I care about and destroy it." The woman came to the realization that the most loving thing she could do for her mother-in-law is to encourage her to be more responsible for herself. Even if this upset the older woman, it would still get her to focus on filling her own needs rather than being angry at her daughter-in-law for filling hers.

This seems to me extremely wise advice. Sometimes people want to hold us back because when we are moving ahead, we are more fully alive. And they are stuck. They can't seem to find a way to grow any more at this point. But we should not cease from flourishing. Sometimes the best thing we can do is to move away from them, allow them some space, and give them the example of a life that is working. One of the greatest gifts you can give your family and friends is to show them a life that works, so they can see it in action and know that it's not just make-believe in the movies.

Chapter 5 — Moodlings

Courage

1.   We have all had moments in our lives when we've said, "I can do that." These may only have been tiny moments, and you may even have forgotten them. But let's look back now and excavate them. When have you done something that amazed you with its boldness, its rightness, its power?

2.   What action have you been afraid to take, now or in the past, for fear of failing?

3.   What steps can you take to give yourself the courage it will take?

4.   Sometimes it is hard to identify courageous acts of our own because we aren't sure what constitutes a truly courageous act. Pick some women that you admire—they can be women you know or public figures, living now or from an earlier time—and identify their acts of courage. Look for acts both big and small—fighting for human rights, or sticking up for a friend under fire. List these acts below.

5.   Now look at the scenarios on this list. What would you have done in these women's shoes?

6.   What absolutely un-you thing would you love to do? If you feel you can't actually do it, describe here what it might be like if you did.

7. What family beliefs have held you back from living the life you'd dreamed about?

8. What family supports have enabled you to try new things and explore your own capabilities? How can you instill these positive ideas in your children and other loved ones so they too will have the courage to be the best selves they can be?

9. Sometimes families don't come with specific creeds or beliefs, or at least no one ever mentioned them to you! So here's an exercise that allows you to pick your own: Write down—or cut out of magazines or photocopy books—every positive motto you can find. If you speak another language, or know someone else who does, don't stop with English— sometimes foreign countries have the best sayings around. When you've found as many as you can, study the list, pick the phrase you like the best (it just has a ring to it that's appealing!) and adopt it as your own for a day. How did living by these words change your behavior? If you like what you see, consider adopting this as *your* motto. If not, try again.

10. Think of five situations in which you wish you'd drawn clearer boundaries. List them here.

11. Take one of the above situations and write out a role-playing dialogue with the other person(s) involved in which you were firm about what you would and wouldn't do. Practice saying your role's dialogue out loud. Do you think you might be able to say it the next time a similar situation arises?

Write Your Way into Wholeness

Passion Will Never Betray Your Trust

It is only by following your deepest instinct that you can lead a rich life and if you let your fear of consequence prevent you from following your deepest instinct, then your life will be safe, expedient and thin.

Katharine Butler Hathaway

Chapter 6

The House of Belonging

*A house is no home unless it
contains food and fire for the mind
as well as for the body.*

MARGARET FULLER

The House of Belonging" is an ancient Celtic metaphor for the human body as the earthly home for the soul. The phrase is also used to describe the deep peace and feeling of safety, joy, and contentment found in intimate soul-friend relationships. John O'Donohue explores this beautiful expression of connection in his *Anam Ċara: A Book of Celtic Wisdom.*

The blueprints of your House of Belonging exist as spiritual energy, hovering above you, ready when you are, to be pulled down from Heaven to shelter your soul on Earth.

"When you learn to love and to let yourself be loved, you come home to the hearth of your own spirit," John O'Donohue declares. "You are warm and sheltered. You are completely at one in the house of your own longing and belonging."

Whenever I have spoken about this feeling of belonging, I have heard from workshop members a collective sigh of yearning. I have come to believe that this desire is one of the deepest we have—the desire to belong, in our own skin, in love, in family, in our work, in our community.

It is difficult in fragmented modern life for many of us to enjoy a sense of community, to feel that we belong. Where do you belong? What are your strongest roots and connections? Would you put belonging to yourself first on the list, or to your family? And then what—a neighborhood or work environment? A community of old friends? Church or temple? What are your Houses of Belonging?

If some of these are lost to you, through divorce, or job displacement, or the death of friends, or from having moved away, what are some ways you can build new connections, as a bird rebuilds a damaged nest?

"The life we want is not merely the one we have chosen and made," the poet Wendell Berry tells us. "It is the one we must be choosing and making." It is ongoing, it is fluid, and just as with a river we can dam it, we can let it flow, we can reroute it, we can swim with it.

Building the House of Belonging is the soul's commitment to living a passionate life, and your Authentic Self is the architect. The timbers with which you build are your choices; courage is the cornerstone; patience, perseverance, and permission are your bricks; faith is the mortar.

A Nest of Comforts

*Ah! there is nothing like staying
at home, for real comfort.*

JANE AUSTEN

I have come to believe that what we want and need most of all in our own homes is to experience a sense of welcome. No matter what our decorating style, the essential spiritual grace that our homes should possess is the solace of comfort. As we discover and express our authenticity through our surroundings, comfort becomes our first priority.

After I began the Simple Abundance path, it shocked me to discover that there were very few places around my home where I felt truly comfortable. I realized I didn't even have a comfortable chair to snuggle into in the living room.

Today, think about your own nest. Is it so cozy that you never want to leave? It should be. Do you have the comforts you crave? Make a wish list: soft, snug places to sit; plump pillows to support or encourage you to take a nap; quilts; a place to put your feet up; proper reading lamps; plenty of bookcases so there's always something on hand that's interesting to read; places to display favorite things.

What's on your wish list?

Think about the rooms in which you have felt instantly at home throughout your life, even if they weren't in your own home. What appealed to you about them and made you want to stay?

The minute we walk into a home, we know whether or not it has charm. There's a coziness that attracts us, a cheerful hospitality. The warm resonance of a charming room beckons us to sink into comfort to our heart's content. Touches of whimsy amuse us. One workshop participant told us that she had been working laboriously on decorating her new apartment, but something indescribable was missing. It was only when a friend gave her the gift of a wonderful small needlepoint rug (showing a happy cat with ball of yarn, mouse, and bird, sitting above the phrase "Home Sweet Home") that she realized her home had lacked a sense of humor. We all need these loving, light touches.

It's important that we be able to comfort ourselves in times of stress. I have what I call my "comfort drawer," but in my New York apartment it's actually a shelf in my linen closet. To create a comfort drawer you can use a shelf, a basket, or an actual drawer. What you put in here are items that spell "relief" and "revive" for you. On those days when we just want to pull the covers over our heads, we need comfort. And we're the only ones who know what we really need.

In your drawer you can put things like bubble bath, favorite photographs, flower-based skin creams. In mine I have special bath oils, French lavender sachets. Then some things that I like to eat—a small box of chocolate truffles, different herbal teas. A couple of English and European fashion magazines that I haven't read. And old love letters, pictures, photographs that mean a lot to me. Scented candles. Favorite CDs I only listen to when I need solace.

Reconsider how caring for our homes can be an expression of our authenticity. . . . creating a comfortable, beautiful, well-run home can be among our most satisfying accomplishments as well as an illuminating spiritual experience.

SIMPLE ABUNDANCE
MAY 8

What goes in *your* comfort drawer?

Some of these items might have to do with sleep, such as herbal melatonin tablets or fabric eyeshades, assuring yourself that you will sleep well. And indeed it is important in eliminating some stress from your life that you get a good night's sleep.

Think about the foods that comforted you when you were sick as a child. Was it chicken noodle soup? Vanilla pudding? In my pantry I have an entire shelf of comfort food, including my favorite brand of cocoa and several boxes of animal crackers. There are just some days when we're feeling so fragile that we need to treat ourselves like babies. We can tell ourselves that we can be taken care of, that we're worth taking care of, that we can provide that care for ourselves. We don't always have to look to someone else to do it.

When you were a child, was there something that comforted you and brought you solace and serenity, a feeling of safety and joy? You may have given this to yourself; in fact, you would not be here reading this book if you hadn't in many ways taken care of yourself, for you wouldn't have survived.

It is important that as we do our excavations we recover for ourselves the things that once brought us joy, comfort, and solace.

Start a file just for comfort food recipes. When you prepare hearty comfort foods, double your pleasure by doubling the recipe to freeze another meal.

Collect soulful recipes, or have someone you love but don't see very often cook for you. Better still, try taking a personal cooking lesson. You might think you know how to make your aunt's jam cake with caramel icing, but do you?

I like to give care packages to people I love; this is one of my greatest joys. I'll put in CDs that I'm listening to, or books that I love. I also send items for their comfort drawers.

One woman in a workshop said that she loves to eat noodles with butter, and I suggested she should add a box of noodles to her comfort drawer—that's comfort food. When in doubt, fettuccini Alfredo never fails.

Comfort can also be taken to your office. Think about all the times when you were caught physically off guard at work—when you needed something and didn't have it, from aspirin to sanitary napkins to an extra pair of stockings or Band-Aids or a sewing kit. Or think of all the times when the office coffeepot just doesn't do the trick, and you long for your favorite herbal tea. Like it or not, you probably spend a lot of time in your office, and having an office comfort drawer means you have a better chance of liking it than not!

Personal Patterns of Peace

Peace—that was the other name for home.

KATHLEEN NORRIS

Now it is time to turn our attention to the third Simple Abundance principle, Order. So with fresh eyes and a loving, appreciative heart, reconsider your life at home.

As you've been going on your creative excursions, have you noticed you've begun to want more order in your life? That's because you've had time and space to figure out what works and what doesn't; without even realizing it, you're bringing order within. This is the first thing that grows out of a desire to simplify your life and to surround yourself only with things you love.

In an attempt to bring order into my own family's life, I began wandering through the rooms of our house, dispassionately observing our patterns of living: how we stored things (or didn't), what areas became catchalls, where we took things out but conveniently forgot to put them back.

I wanted to bring more order into my life, because quite frankly I got tired of opening up the kitchen cabinets to an avalanche of margarine tubs that we saved for leftovers. It was a little thing, to be sure. But as the writer Fannie Fern so astutely observed, "There are no little things. Little things are the hinges of the universe."

Simplicity does not mean making do with less, but

appreciating the important things more. It means making deliberate decisions to surround yourself only with objects that inspire, comfort, soothe, and serve you. Paring down to those essentials is more than just cleaning, organizing, or rearranging. Clearing away the clutter is a spiritual endeavor made up of choices, not chores, and the process itself can be as satisfying and empowering as the results: With every decision, you are creating a calm, clear space for yourself. You are making room for wonderful new gifts to come into your life, such as order, serenity, and creativity.

Choose any room in your home, sit down, and close your eyes. When you open them a few quiet moments later, imagine that you are seeing everything around you for the first time. Are you looking at a harmonious blend of beautiful objects, or an unruly jumble? Most likely, there's a bit of both. Our rooms are filled with complex combinations of the things we love but take for granted, and the things we don't love but have learned to live with—and sometimes it's even hard to remember which is which. Why? Because it's time to simplify.

Continue to take in your surroundings from a fresh perspective and with simplicity in mind. Spend time in each room, giving every piece of furniture or decorative accessory your full attention. Ask yourself if each object is beautiful, useful, or genuinely rich in sentimental value. If it doesn't meet one of those criteria, let it go. This will teach you a lot about your possessions and about yourself. Perhaps you'll realize that you're collecting teacups out of habit, not passion. Or that the delicate piece of art

Sarah Ban Breathnach

Begin to think of order not as a strait-jacket of "should" (make the bed, wash the dishes, take out the garbage) but as a shape—the foundation— for the beautiful new life you are creating.

SIMPLE ABUNDANCE
JANUARY 16

glass doesn't give you enough joy to balance the time it takes to dust it. Be candid; don't try to convince yourself that you love something because you used to or because your mother gave it to you. Accept how you've changed, and discover what it is that you love now.

Now apply the same standards to all of those things lurking in closets and drawers and cupboards— once you summon the strength to face them.

What are your most essential pieces? What would you mourn if it disappeared? (Hint: If you have more than six essential possessions, rethink the word "essential.")

Once you've taken inventory, make appointments with yourself to bring order to your daily round. It's important to write them down on the calendar. Plan to work on only one room per month; within that room, plan to conquer one area a week. Clearing a single closet, junk drawer, craft cupboard, or medicine chest is an accomplishment in itself. This methodical approach means committing to simplifying, and prevents you from feeling overwhelmed. And don't sabotage your efforts for lack of the right supplies. Collect cardboard boxes from supermarkets, consider investing in big plastic bins for seasonal storage, and have some garbage bags—yes, garbage bags—on hand. If buying a set of sturdy clothes hangers to replace the tangled wire ones will make you feel more content with your closet, do it (just look for some on sale!).

As you make your way through a room or closet or drawer, sort all the items into piles according to their destiny. You will unearth some things that go straight into a garbage bag; do not even attempt to keep the ancient makeup, worn-out batteries, and all manner of broken gadgets that weren't so helpful even when they worked. But much of what you no longer have room for could be loved by someone else. Being creative in the ways of giving, of sharing the "simple abundance" that surrounds you, does not cost money.

Your friend who loves to bake will be thrilled to receive the animal-shaped cookie cutters you've never used; another will be delighted to inherit your maternity clothes. And of course, your local thrift shops, the Salvation Army, Goodwill, the Red Cross, churches and synagogues, and shelters for the homeless will all be grateful for your donations. If you have books or computer equipment to spare, contact libraries or schools. If you clear out your pantry, take the excess to a food bank.

Carefully consider the areas of your home that are causing you the most frustration today, in order of annoyance:

When in doubt, throw it away. No, it will not come in handy someday. Every cleared junk drawer, each closet, each successful attempt at organizing, only reinforces your feeling of taking back control of your life.

And after all that, what remains before you are the beautiful, useful, and meaningful objects that speak to your soul. Now you can listen to them.

In this way you can find the breathing space you crave. You may think you're only clearing clutter from a junk drawer or juggling commitments to find a few hours to get your house in order. But your soul knows better.

An artist knows that there must be order in which to create. You can't be painting a masterpiece if you go to your easel and all your brushes are dried up with paint on them. There is sublime order in the Universe and there should be sublime order in our lives too. I believe that at the end of the day, if you walk into your living room and you can't find a place to sit down and collect yourself, the Universe is sending you a cosmic SOS. *Simplify. Order. Simplify.*

Rumer Godden, in her book *A House with Four Rooms,* writes of the soulcraft of creating and sustaining safe havens, set apart from the world, in which to seek and savor small authentic joys. Her secret to living an authentic life seems to have been dwelling, no matter where she actually kept house, in the House of Spirit. "There is an Indian proverb or axiom that says that everyone is a house with four rooms, a physical, a mental, an emotional and a spiritual," she tells us. "Most of us tend to live in one room most of the time, but unless we go into every room every day even if only to keep it aired, we are not a complete person."

Once when I was in my thirties I was intrigued to hear a conversation among some women, all in their fifties, at a party. We were in the kitchen, and these women were talking about a dream that several of them had had—that they were back in the home of their childhood but that the house had more rooms than they remembered, more nooks and crannies and wings.

I have never forgotten that conversation, and in fact I've now had the dream myself. I like to think that it means our lives are bigger, our personalities more expansive, than we have realized. There is more space for us, more diversity, more possibility in our lives than we have grasped.

Making use of all of our space is a bit like trying to write with your left hand (or your right, if you're left-handed). We tend to use the same muscles over and over again; we tend to sit in the same places in our homes. But if we can go to a new, perhaps neglected corner, we can also perhaps reach into a neglected corner of our minds. It reminds me of how Lady Bird Johnson was said to spend time in each of her guest rooms, sleeping in the beds, making sure they would be comfortable for her visitors.

Today, go to a room or a part of a room in which you rarely spend time. Why is this so? Is it "dead space"?

How can you make it more alive? Add a plant? Move a chair, turn a chair to a different angle? Put in a lamp?

Gradually, as I have moved along the Simple Abundance path, I have discovered that I've outgrown many of the objects that lived in my home for years, and my Authentic Self has yet to reveal what should take their place, if anything. It's difficult for many of us to accept that emptiness—in life or in a living room—can have a positive influence. I think we need to learn how to tolerate more empty space. We need either to become more comfortable with waiting to fill what's empty with what is authentic, or just to become willing to accept the exquisite fullness of nothing. Life's landscape becomes a lot more interesting when we realize there is an entire dimension we've never considered before, simply because we couldn't see it.

What you're inviting is your authenticity to express itself through your surroundings, one object at a time. You might like to create some empty spaces in your home to jump-start your ability to see things in a new light. Believe me, you will be energized. There'll be no going back.

Move some furniture out of a room. Take pictures

off a wall. Clear off tabletops. Experience the fullness of nothing for a while. Then pretend that you've just moved into a new home. Don't be surprised if the woman you are becoming reveals that she needs more space in which to grow.

When an artist prepares to draw or paint, she carefully considers the balance between "positive shapes" and "negative spaces." The negative spaces surround the objects and define them with a boundary. The space surrounding the bowl of fruit is as important as the bowl itself if Wholeness is to emerge. To the oriental mind, the empty space is pregnant with possibilities. Not only is the round glass vase that holds the spring flowers beautiful, so is the empty space surrounding the vase, accentuating its pleasing form. That "negative space" delineates the vase, draws our eye to it, in a sense holds it.

Just as in a Quaker meeting, where people sit in silence, the silence is not "dead," it is living. A nurturing silence, full of possibility.

As you awaken to your authenticity, you may notice that bare walls, windows, and floors beckon invitingly like a new lover.

Let Love Be Your Decorator

*Perhaps loving something is the only starting place
there is for making your life your own.*

ALICE KOLLER

We can't all begin from scratch with an empty
house or apartment and refurnish it all at
once. But we can start the weeding process, getting rid of
things we can't stand, opening up some space.

Is there a woman alive who doesn't long to live in a
home that embraces, nurtures, sustains, and inspires? You
think it can't happen here? Don't look at the problems,
search for the possibilities. Learn love's decorating secrets.

Before you pick up a hammer, paintbrush, or the real
estate ads, you need to daydream. Walk through the different rooms where you eat, sleep, and live. Bless the
walls, the roof, the windows, and the foundation. Realize
that the home of your dreams dwells within.

Continue to prime the well, pasting visual images
into your Illustrated Discovery Journal, collecting everything you can on paper, from fabulous table settings to
beautiful curtain treatments.

Get ready. Experiment. Observe. Embark on creative
window-shopping excursions. Check newspapers for estate and moving sales, scan grocery store bulletin boards
for flea market announcements.

Foraging at such sales and in thrift shops gives us
the ability to view the old and abandoned in a new

light—to reclaim things from oblivion with creativity and choice, just as we do the days of our lives—and to redeem them with love.

If you follow these suggestions, you'll be well on your way to developing and nurturing your authentic flair. Instead of being frustrated, you'll be grateful that you have been given the extraordinary gift of time—time to know what you love so you can love how you live.

When in doubt, live without. Because you can. If you don't get a visceral response to something new and you can walk away from it, you're meant to because it's not meant for you. There is an expression, "What is mine will know my face," meaning that what is yours is seeking you. If you make space in your life for it, whether it's a new sofa or relationship, it will find you.

As I began to pare down my possessions and edit my belongings, I started feeling lighter. My rooms felt more spacious. There was suddenly an expansiveness of possibility; this is what abundance feels like. I was coming home to contentment.

The homes we grow up in and the homes that we become grown-ups in are not meant to be the same. In my own case, my evolving decorating style went from American Country, to Victorian, and then English Cottage. While all three of these decorating styles have their charm, they didn't really reflect the true me. And while the rooms worked, they felt like stage sets. Gradually, as I worked through the pages of my Illustrated Discovery Journal, I noticed that I kept pasting images from the Arts and Crafts movement (1890s), Mission (1910), and

There is an immediate emotional and psychological payoff to getting our houses in order. We might not be able to control what's happening externally in our lives but we can learn to look to our inner resources for a sense of comfort that nurtures and sustains.

SIMPLE ABUNDANCE
JANUARY 16

135

Art Deco (1930s). They blended well on paper, so I invited them to mesh in my living room. And it works.

Why? Because I love each individual piece. Every chair, table, and vase elicited an emotional response when I saw it; they still do every day.

The things you love should trigger an emotional response. If you need it, if you want it, if you love it, it will let you know that. And that goes for new relationships too.

Not every one of our desires can be immediately gratified. Nor should they. Why? Because we need to prepare a place symbolically for our hopes and dreams. Start by making sure there's room for that new thing or new person that you would like in your life, both in your home and in your heart. What has your Illustrated Discovery Journal led you to think such a thing or such a person might be?

Color Your Life Beautiful

What kind of green? Green like my bottles? Green like a grasshopper? Green like a cucumber, lettuce, or green like the sky just before it breaks loose to storm?

TONI MORRISON

"Color is the cheapest and easiest form of change," the designer and writer Alexandra Stoddard tells us. When life is dreary and drab it's time to introduce more color into your daily round.

We all have "color memories," according to Ms. Stoddard. Her first color memory was when she was three years old, sitting in her mother's garden and discovering for the first time the different colors of the flowers. A friend's first color memory came as a schoolgirl when she was given a beautiful tangerine blouse. My most vibrant color memory arrived as a teenager when my mother painted our living room red long before it was fashionable to do.

What were the colors of your childhood? What colors were in your bedroom? What color was your favorite in the Crayola box? List your "comfort colors" here.

Was there a moment when you really saw color for the first time? As you think back, consider Ms. Stoddard's reflection that "beautiful colors are not out there: they are inside our brains, in our minds, experienced in our hearts, and then seen through our eyes."

Last summer a friend and I visited the little cabin of a couple in Maine. We arrived in a driving rainstorm, having crossed the lake in an open boat. We were drenched when we entered the cabin. But a fire glowed in the fireplace, and the little round table was set, with pretty turquoise placemats, napkins and silver, flowers at the center, a bottle of wine, along with a raspberry tart that our hostess had baked for us. I have rarely felt so welcome and so quickly restored.

When you take extra moments to prepare an attractive table, you're really performing an invocation, welcoming Spirit to be present in re-creation and remembrance. Choosing to dine rather than just to eat is a small but significant step toward self-nurturance, and one to savor. Creating an inviting table is possible more nights than you might think, especially if you approach it as another form of artistic expression in your daily round.

In thinking about your home and your life, "Put your preconceptions of what should and shouldn't go together away—do exactly the opposite of what your old sense would tell you and you will find yourself in a whole new creative landscape," artist Judyth van Amringe tells us in her book *Home Art: Creating Romance and Magic with Everyday Objects.* "Here is the challenge," she says. "To turn a piece around, rework it, make it totally your own, your style, your signature."

Today, start using and enjoying the beautiful things that already surround you in your home. Don't save their loveliness only for other people to recognize and appreciate. What things would these be? What odd and charming things can you use to hold your pencils, your spatulas, your flowers? The marvelous is always waiting to be revealed behind the unexpected.

Chapter 6 — Moodlings

The House of Belonging

1. *Determine your housekeeping livability quotient.* This is the first step toward devising a personal plan that will work for you. Rank your requirements (for example, you can't live with dishes in the sink, but you can put up with dusty bookshelves):

2. Next, figure out what daily or weekly chores need to be done, who can do them, and when:

Chore   *When*

3. We can't afford to put our lives and creativity on hold until there's more cash on hand. What's stopping you from making the changes that would make you happier in your home?

In what ways could you compensate for these?

4.   Think about the time when you set up your first home. Where was it? How was it furnished? Are you still living with some of your early decorating choices? Do they reflect who you are now or have you outgrown them? Which items still make you feel good when you use or look at them? List them here:

5.   Imagine you have an empty house to fill—list ten "must-haves":

6.   What are your first color memories? Was there a moment when you really *saw* color for the first time? This could be as basic as seeing that a brighter pink makes your face glow, or as complex as noticing the way Picasso's color scheme is different from that of Matisse. Whatever the experience, describe it below:

7.   Every life has its gray spaces, and gray days. How can you bring more beauty into your life in simple, colorful ways?

8.   Does a certain smell or taste make memories come flooding back? Or a song, a piece of music? William Styron describes in his brilliant memoir of depression, *Darkness Visible,* how it was hearing a beloved passage from Brahms that brought him back to himself and saved his life. What powerful talismans trigger memories in you?

9.   What objects do you love and perhaps collect without even realizing it? What favorite things have you accumulated over the years that you now lovingly display around your home?

10.   If you haven't acted on a passion for collecting until now, what would you like to collect if you had the chance?

Write Your Way into Wholeness

You, As Well As God, Are Found in the Details

I find you in all small and lovely things; in the little fishes like flames in the green water, in the furred and stupid softness of the bumble-bees fat as laughter, in all the chiming radiance of warmth and light and scent in the summer garden.

Winifred Holtby

Choice As a Spiritual Gift

Such creatures of accident are we,
liable to a thousand deaths before we are born.
But once we are here, we may create our
own world, if we choose.

MARY ANTIN

In both *Something More* and *Simple Abundance* I spoke about the phenomenon of "Divine Discontent." We know that personal growth comes in spurts: three steps forward, two steps back, and then a long plateau when it seems as though nothing is happening. The dormant period always seems to precede a growth spurt. Unfortunately, during the dormant period we often become depressed and decide to give up.

Divine Discontent happens as you are about to move into harmony. By this I mean: you hate the way you look. You hate your clothes, you hate the meals you are cooking. You hate your home. You may even start to hate the people around you. You are so dissatisfied with your life that you feel this process is not working; you believe you're worse off than you were six months ago.

But hold on. This is working. This is the grain of sand

Sarah Ban Breathnach

Live your questions.
Then ask. Become
open to the changes that
the answers will
inevitably bring.

SIMPLE ABUNDANCE
JANUARY 2

in the oyster that produces the pearl. William Butler Yeats talks in his poem "The Second Coming" about the center not holding. And he's right. Perhaps your center *is* about to fall out from beneath you. But maybe it was a false center, one that could not have supported you through your entire life. Now you have started to dismantle all the illusions that held it together, and you're wobbly with worry. But you have to go through this stage or you will not get your second wind, your second booster thrust.

I once spoke with a very spiritual woman who warned me that anytime it seems like you are getting where you are supposed to be, anytime you seem to be making strides, suddenly a seemingly benign dark force appears that can easily derail your progress.

I'm talking about the little things, the second-guessing, the undermining, the mischief makers that pop up in your life. Can you pinpoint these influences in your life?

The hallmark of Divine Discontent is that everything is out of kilter, there is no balance. Psychically you're so shaky you're accident-prone.

This is good news, but unless you know it's good, when you wake up and don't have a thing you can put on that you like, when the thought of going to the same old job depresses you—those things will throw you. Spiritual growth is like living on a fault line.

So hold on and rejoice when Divine Discontent kicks in, because you are exactly where you're supposed to be.

Think of Divine Discontent as your pre-magnificent stage.

Courageous Choices, Authentic Lives

In true courage there is always an element of choice . . . and of anguish, and also of action and deed. There is always a flame of spirit in it, a vision of some necessity higher than oneself.

BRENDA UELAND

As you trace your life, reflect on the choices you have made. Have they been the right ones for you? Do you choose with your heart, mind, or gut? Are you comfortable with your style of choosing?

Both authenticity and adventure require a point of departure, the willingness to shed what's safe and predictable in order to embrace the *new*—people, places, predicaments, pleasures, and passions. Your new, authentic life.

Choices—day in, day out—shape your destiny. There

147

are only three ways to change the trajectory of our lives—crisis, chance, and choice. Your life at this exact moment is a direct result of choices you made once upon a time.

Our choices can be conscious or unconscious. Conscious choice is creative, the heart of authenticity. Unconscious choice is destructive, the heel of self-abuse (as in, "I can't marry this man because then I will break my bond with my parents." "I can't move away from this town / leave this company / leave my childhood home / leave this marriage because then who will I be?"). Unconscious choice is how we end up living other people's lives.

Make a conscious choice every day to shed the old. Old issues, old guilt, old patterns, which may involve habits of eating or drinking, patterns of responding, of suppressing anger, old resentments, old rivalries.

This is the emotional baggage we want to shed. This is all that stands between your dream of living authentically and its coming true.

Most women are petrified of making choices, because we don't trust our instincts. But we, not our outer circumstances, are the catalysts for the quality of our lives. Luckily, our lives are not entirely shaped by wrong or bad choices. There have been wise choices, good choices, strong choices, courageous choices, happy choices. Brilliant decisions. Sometimes we make a decision quickly, with our hearts—as in falling in love with the first house we see, when we're househunting. And then our heads take over, analyzing, second-guessing. ("How can you buy this? You're supposed to look around!")

Ask for what you need and want. Ask to be taught the right questions. Ask to be answered. Ask for the Divine Plan of your life to unfold through joy. Ask politely. Ask with passion. Ask with a grateful heart and you will be heard.

SIMPLE ABUNDANCE
JUNE 3

148

So it should hardly be surprising if sometimes our initial reaction is to avoid making a choice, to put it off as long as possible. But by not choosing, we allow others to decide for us.

"You make what seems a simple choice: choose a man or a job or a neighborhood," Jessamyn West muses. "However, what you have chosen is not a man or a job or a neighborhood, but a life."

Can you think of a time when your life dramatically changed because of one small choice that seemed simple?

What are three small choices or changes you could make now, to begin to enhance your life in big ways? Eat two-thirds of what you customarily eat, to begin to lose weight? Spend one-third less than you usually spend, to save money? Read a singles ad, or write one? Take a four-mile walk? Go to the store and look at new rugs? Speak to a stranger? Roll out of bed in the morning and run around the block? What would you like to do that is new and different?

Little choices count a lot. In fact, little ones can often be more life-altering than big ones.

Small Changes

One can never change the past,
only the hold it has on you.

MERLE SHAIN

The first time you think you'd like to do something a little differently from the way you've always done it, you pick up a pebble. The first time you actually do it differently, you throw the pebble into the pond. The pebble sends out tiny, barely visible ripples of movement toward the edges. No one else notices. But the woman who threw the pebble does if she's paying attention. A friend of mine is a college professor and normally a conservative dresser, but one night she appeared at a casual dinner party with friends wearing a rhinestone-studded cardigan. I don't know if others picked up on this the way I did, but to me my friend seemed to be sending a signal: I am not the dull woman you think. I am coming out of my shell. I am a beautiful, sexy woman! And do you know what? She is.

It's the same way with courageous choices in your daily round. One day, all of your small but indelible moments of private courage will burst through. And both you and your world will have changed in an authentic moment.

We become authentic the same way we become courageous. By doing it.

Most of us are hungering for something more in our lives. Admitting that you want something more is the first step in starting over.

The way to take giant leaps and strides toward our authenticity is through small changes. When your heart is open to change, you're able to recognize the personal signals of encouragement that your Authentic Self is constantly sending.

I met a woman who told me that as she's gotten older, she has decided that being "bold" will keep her from later saying to herself, "If only I had had the courage to try for what I wanted." Seizing opportunities and taking risks can ensure that we don't look back on a life of regrets.

As we look for a new job, a new love, a new home, new friends, we barely know where these new things will present themselves or the forms they will take. So we take a leap of faith, tell friends what we're looking for, get the energy going, and try to be open to receive. In my experience the answers aren't likely to come from the sources we expect; but they *will* come from the cycle of positive energy we've set in motion.

Before making major decisions or choices, I also take my questions to the spiritual world for consultation. For three nights in a row, just before I go to sleep, I ask my question. I remember learning this early—a

You have to know what you need and want out of life before you can make the choices necessary to honor them.

SOMETHING MORE
"SOMETHING MORE"

teacher in the seventh grade told us that if we were struggling with a math problem we could put it aside and come back to it later that day or the next morning. The answer—or at least an approach to it—might then be clear, because our subconscious mind continues to work on the problem while we're away from it.

Change happens a choice at a time. We shape our lives through choices we make every day. Above all, being open to change helps. Welcome it.

What recent changes did you perhaps block, or resist? How can you be more open to change?

Only Ask

*Strange, when you ask anyone's advice
you see yourself what is right.*

SELMA LAGERLÖF

There is something that has brought a sense of adventure to my daily round: it's *asking* for what I want. Help. Advice. Wisdom. Guidance. Information—especially information. We want, we need, we desire, we yearn, but we don't ask. "We make requests of our fellow creatures as well as God: we ask for the salt, we ask for a raise in pay, we ask a friend to feed the cat while we are on holidays," the English writer C. S. Lewis observed. "Sometimes we get what we ask for and sometimes not. But when we do, it is not nearly as easy to prove . . . [the] causal connection between the asking and the getting."

I was always envious of a friend who could ask for things easily. She was forced to learn to do this, because when she was a teenager she contracted polio and was left with a twisted spine. She *had* to declare what she wanted. Another friend, a man, also finds it easy to ask for what he needs. He wants to meet a new woman, and he simply asks friends about women they might know. He asks if he can stay with family when he is traveling. He asks colleagues to critique a speech he's going to give. He's a happy man. Why? He says because he chooses to ask for what he needs.

Asking for help is a choice. But many of us don't ask because we're afraid somebody will say no. We choose not to ask, but we continue to wish, existing in a state of deprivation. Asking comes with no guarantees. But I know that if we don't ask, we haven't got a prayer.

Today, start asking for what you want. Ask your husband to take the kids for the afternoon to give you some time to yourself. Ask the kids to pick up the toys so that you don't have to do it. Ask for a deadline extension. Ask for the day off. Ask for a raise. Ask Spirit for a daily portion of grace. Ask for what you need and want. Ask to be taught the right questions. Ask to be an-

Our choices can be conscious or unconscious. Conscious choice is creative, the heart of authenticity. Unconscious choice is destructive, the heel of self-abuse. Unconscious choice is how we end up living other people's lives.

SOMETHING MORE
"DESIGNING WOMEN"

swered. Ask with a grateful heart and you will be heard. Just ask. What will you ask for?

The only thing that is constant in our lives and in the world is change. Yet we get frightened and "stay in the box" because we fear change. I am a woman who had to be pulled, kicking and screaming, into her absolutely fabulous destiny, because I was so afraid of change. So even if you knew that one year from today you could be living your life exactly as you wanted it—the life you dream of—you would still be frightened because it would mean change. Remember, what we call chaos, Heaven calls change.

Chapter 7 — Moodlings

Choices As a Spiritual Gift

1.   If you had all of your financial needs satisfied, all of your responsibilities taken care of, the freedom to do *anything* you wanted . . . what would you do? What are the aspirations of your heart?

2.   What talent have you yearned for that would make your life richer? Could it be those talents are already within you?

3.   What dreams and talents do you possess right now that you are nurturing, tending, allowing to flourish?

4.   If you could be instantly brilliant at one particular practical task, what would that be? Why?

5.   If you had three things you could change about your life, what would they be?

6.   If you could change three things about yourself, what would they be?

7.   How would your choices be different if you were a man?

8. When you look back on your life, and you are told that you can only take the good with you, what will you take?

9. What are the blocks that have kept you from asking for the things you need—from your family, your friends, your employer, yourself?

10. Skeptics make the best seekers. Is there a choice or decision you're wrestling with? Try sleeping on it. Write it down in a simple sentence on a small slip of paper. Before you go to sleep, read it aloud to yourself, then slip it in your pillowcases. Do this three nights in a row. On the fourth morning, don't bolt out of bed. Wait a few minutes and mull over your choice. See if you don't have more clarity, or at least a strong intuition about the next step.

Write Your Way into Wholeness

The Joy of Getting What You Want Instead of Having It All

There must be more to life than having everything.

Maurice Sendak

Chapter 8

The Love of Play

The creation of something new is not accomplished by the intellect but by the play instinct acting from inner necessity. The creative mind plays with the objects it loves.

C. G. JUNG

Remember, once upon a time, when we all knew how to play? We're going to have to travel back to when we were younger to look for clues about how to resume this soul-nurturing pastime.

Sometimes grown women need to be reminded not only how to play, but also of the sacredness of play. In her luminous meditation on the importance of enchantment in our lives, *Deep Play,* Diane Ackerman explores the nature of the state of transcendence accessed only through play. "For humans, play is refuge from life's customs, methods, and decrees. . . . Play is an activity enjoyed for its own sake. It is our brain's favorite way of learning and maneuvering. . . . It gives us the opportunity to perfect ourselves. It's organic to who and what we are, a process as instinctive as breathing."

What was your favorite game in childhood? Jump rope? Hide-and-seek? Playing kick-the-can at dusk? Putting on plays? Climbing trees? Playing with dolls?

What was your favorite sport? Tennis? Swimming? Baseball? What was the best time you ever had when

159

When you embark on creative excursions, your authentic self will lovingly reveal to you the beautiful mystery that is you. This occurs spontaneously as you make the pursuit of personal growth a sacred endeavor.

SIMPLE ABUNDANCE
FEBRUARY 1

you were young? Camping with your family? With the Girl Scouts? Learning folk dancing? Going to the prom? Cheerleading?

When I started my own personal excavation and began to go back into my past, I really wanted to bring into my life some emotional talismans from childhood. For example, I tried to find a tiny carved apple that was similar to the one given to me on a special vacation with my family when I was a child. I wanted to be able to touch such memories because it's not enough for us to travel back emotionally; we need to do it physically as well. That's why you need the feeling of dipping into finger paints after all these years, or even the smell of Vicks VapoRub. Tactile moments spiritually induce the trip back to our true self.

So for a long time as an adult, I've always been on the lookout for a carved apple. And while I've never exactly re-created the one of my memory, another holds its place—similar but different, like the days of our lives. It now stands on what I call my "play shelf."

You too can start a play shelf, or a small corner where you can keep some of the delights of your childhood. Can you remember the smell of Play-Doh? When was the last time you opened a new box of crayons with all sixty-four colors? That was major excitement for me—and I loved that it came with a sharpener to keep my crayons fresh. Get yourself a box of deluxe crayons and put it on your desk or wherever you have a special place. The mere presence of such a beloved creative tool of childhood can do wonders to jump-start your dormant sense of play.

On my play shelf I keep a little sheep beanbag, a collection of rubber wonder women, a wind-up man, a Mr. Peanut can filled with marbles. You could also keep jacks and a ball, paper dolls, travel-size board games, a Nancy Drew or Hardy Boys mystery, a deck of fortune-telling cards. Include things that you used to enjoy playing with, and that people in your home would enjoy playing with now—even your big burly male guests.

What might you keep on your play shelf?

A spirit of spontaneity can fill your home with fun. Often the home that best expresses its owner's authentic sense of style is decorated with a lighthearted touch. It possesses that spark of high spirits that tells you good times are part of this home's personal history.

If you didn't really have a childhood, if you had to take care of others and weren't really allowed to be a child, you can experience that childhood now. You can give yourself permission to play.

One of the benefits of play is that we moved our bodies, whether we hung from trees, played Red Rover, or swung from monkey bars. We leaped on hopscotch squares, swam, played in the water. Built forts. Part of what made us happy was that our bodies were in motion. Getting exercise, using our sense of physical coordination—these are exhilarating feelings, and we need to reclaim this exhilaration.

The soul of passionate play is imagination. We could sit and fashion paper-napkin wedding dresses for our dolls, we could imagine ourselves navigating a raft down the Mississippi, or crossing the wide plains toward our own "Little House on the Prairie" in a turned-over card table.

How did you and your friends use your imagination in play? What ordinary objects became magical? A basket? A chair? A blanket? And how did you use them in play? Who played with you? What are your best memories? (Mine was an elaborately orchestrated Tom Thumb wedding in which, of course, I was the beautiful bride.)

Did you play school? A friend of mine made up stories about her marbles, turning them into families: a mother, father, children, who had adventures. My brothers, sister, and I pretended to be cowgirls and Indians. I was always ready to be a famous movie star in dark glasses and a large hat of my mother's.

Kids aren't the only ones who have permission to revel in their imaginations. You do too. Start by writing. Or painting. By making pottery. By designing and shaping a room, a home. By singing, by giving voice. By making home movies. If you could do anything playful, right at this minute, what would it be?

It is said that you shouldn't go into a profession if you don't enjoy playing with its artifacts—greasepaint and costumes; fabrics and textiles; canvas and tubes of paint; leotards; stethoscopes; clay. If you love the trappings of a profession, you are likely to love the profession itself. You can play with these artifacts, you can play with the lines of a poem, you can play with the clay as you shape the pot.

My sister, Maureen, who is a brilliant businesswoman, is also a gifted artisan, especially with creating dollhouse miniatures. For years she permitted herself to "play" by creating a breathtaking but tiny version of her dream house. Her Victorian dollhouse was a psychic placeholder for her House of Belonging. For a few years, as her life became more complicated, she stopped playing in her parallel world because she didn't have time. Recently, though, she realized that she accomplished more at work when playtime was a regular part of her routine. She's back at it now, and her latest triumph is a miniscule cornucopia complete with fruits and vegetables.

Through play we can find ways to renew and replenish ourselves. An artist friend, Daisy, told me that she was concerned about how rigid and predictable her paintings had become. But the more she tried to remedy the situation, the more control she tried to exert on her creativity, the more dull and lifeless her paintings were.

One day she visited a neighbor who is a potter. The potter was brushing glaze onto her clay pots before firing them. She invited Daisy to join her.

What happened then was a breakthrough for my talented friend. She freely brushed some glaze onto a pot and put it in the oven. When it was done, she saw that the glaze had formed its own beautiful pattern, one that had been out of her control. Feeling elated, Daisy asked the potter if she could "help out" for the next few weeks.

This experience freed her. She went back to her own work feeling liberated, not choking the life out of her paintings with control. Instead she allowed herself to be a catalyst for the creative energy moving through her, to her brush, to the canvas. From that time on, her paintings took on a freedom and depth and mystery that had never been there before.

How can you bring such cross-fertilization into your own life? Just as crops need to be rotated, so does the soil of our souls. How about putting your tools aside—your computer, your cookbook, your sewing machine, your calculator—and going out for a walk? Do you type? Try hand-writing your letters instead of using e-mail. If you are doing needlepoint, sweep the porch. If you are working at a desk, do tai chi or yoga. If you are obsessively weeding in your garden, come in and do a crossword puzzle. Play baseball with your children. Go square dancing. Bird-watch. Forget following the instructions of a recipe and rustle up a culinary experiment from your imagination.

What can be your pottery-and-glaze experience?

I know there are things you absolutely must do every day. But try to bring a sense of play to your work. Snow White had it right: the daily drudgery goes faster if you whistle while you work. You can cook to music, boogie while you're cleaning, try weeding your garden with a child. Make it play, make it a game.

Do you have a hobby? A hobby provides that wonderful middle ground between work and play; you give it more weight than play and yet it doesn't have the seriousness of work. Truth be told, we all secretly wish that our hobbies could be our work!

A hobby affords us a marvelous opportunity to awaken our buried talents and illuminates our natural inclinations. That's because no one expects us to be perfect at a hobby. Hobbies allow us to experiment, to dabble. We get to try on imaginary lives and see how they fit.

A friend named Doris told me that when she was thirty she was astonished at how difficult it was to play with her toddler, especially if the game meant sitting on the floor. She began to realize that she was terribly out of shape and she'd better do something about it.

Women are artists of the everyday. The world does not acknowledge or applaud everyday art, so we must. We are the keepers of a sacred truth. We must cherish this wisdom and pass it on to those we love.

SIMPLE ABUNDANCE
AUGUST 29

She usually spent her workday sitting at a desk. A modern dance class was being given at the local YWCA, and she enrolled, thinking, "I'm an adult. I don't have to stay, I can walk out anytime I want." And furthermore, "I'm not a professional dancer. No one expects me to be good at this."

Twenty years later, she's still taking modern dance classes. She's using another part of her brain, her body is more flexible, and the class serves as a new way to express her emotions. It keeps her energy flowing and brings her joy. Now, in her early fifties, she's more flexible than she was when her baby was born.

If you can approach some things with a *this really doesn't count; it's just practice* attitude, and remind yourself that no one is keeping score, it can take off some of the pressure. The secret is not to put unnecessary demands on yourself.

Creative Excursions

Give me books, fruit, French wine and fine weather and a little music out of doors, played by someone I do not know. . . . I admire lolling on a lawn by a water-lilied pond to eat white currants and see goldfish.

JOHN KEATS

If we are to flourish as creative beings, if we are to grow into Wholeness, we must learn to play happily in our own backyards. Right now, you might not

Joy is where your life began, with your first cry. Joy is your birthright.

SOMETHING MORE
"WHEN THE
STUDENT IS READY"

have the perfect career, home, or relationship. Few of us do. But if you have the gift of today, you've got another chance to re-create your circumstances and make them as perfect as possible with the resources you do have. Every day you get another chance to get it as right as you can make it. Creative excursions help. You know how important it is for us to schedule play dates for your children? It's the same way for their mothers.

Creative excursions don't have to cost money; they're simply things you've never done, or haven't done in a long time. Have you been dying to go to an art exhibit? Try on new clothes? Get a pedicure? Explore a different part of town? Go for a hike? Call an old friend and meet for tea downtown? Visit a botanical garden? Look at items to be sold at an auction house? Check out a local health-food store? Go online and surf the Web?

On my first creative excursion I visited an art supply store and just walked around. I am not a fine artist, and I can't create magical things with my hands, but I love the visual. I just walked around to see all of the different media I could use to express myself—colored pencils and pens, sketchbooks and canvases of all sizes, pastels, colored clay, paints.

I went to fabric stores and rummaged through the upholstery remnant table and found great pieces of fabric that could be made into tablecloths, pillows, and simple curtains.

I went to the cosmetic counter at a department store and tried a new red lipstick. The next week I had a cappuccino at a café and began a new mystery. I went alone to a movie I'd seen reviewed that nobody else wanted to see.

These excursions were very simple, but very self-nurturing. And after about three weeks I began to get an even stronger sense of other things I wanted to do. The world was my oyster and it only took two hours a week!

Make a list now of some things you'd love to do, if you were given some free time in each of the next three weeks:

Week 1

Week 2

Week 3

These creative excursions are regular rendezvous with your Authentic Self. So find pastimes that make your heart light and your spirit sing. You might want to join a choir, study Latin, walk around in a neighboring town, muse by a river, roll out of bed in the morning and do stretches, then have an early breakfast at a diner before you go to work. Explore a fabulous thrift shop; go to a crafts museum. Nurturing our imaginations and developing a relationship with our Authentic Selves is an investment we can no longer afford to put off.

Arrange a creative excursion to go browsing in a home furnishings and decorative accessories shop. Go somewhere you've never been before, so that you look at everything with fresh eyes. What calls to you? Is it the texture of a hooked rug, the tile pattern of a fabulous restaurant ladies' room, the warm glow of a pine chest? You'll know what you love the moment you see it. Trust the impulse, record the clues. Do the same with a clothing boutique. Go not to buy, just to browse. Which colors and patterns entrance you? Note them here, or record them in a small spiral notebook that you can keep in your purse:

It's important to plan your creative excursions ahead of time. I know how hard it is to block out those two hours, so you want to use them well.

Transformation is really what we are seeking when we desire to commune with our Authentic Selves. This week keep a date with that someone special. Keep a date with You.

Chapter 8 — Moodlings

The Love of Play

1. Archaeologists, with their keen powers of observation and curiosity, must have the ability to recognize patterns. Let's decode some of the messages of the things that have made you happy in the past and that you may have forgotten—your holidays or trips that first spoke to you as a young girl.

Think of your three favorite trips. Is there a pattern? Is it the place? The way you traveled? Your traveling companions? Where you stayed?

What is your favorite holiday? How did you celebrate it? What decorations do you remember? How was the table set for the holiday meal?

2. What was your favorite souvenir? What was your favorite holiday gift?

3. Create a box of "Firsts" to generate new ideas for your creative excursions. Each week when you read the newspaper or a magazine and you see something you've never tried before but would like to, just tear it out and put it in your box of Firsts. This could be anything—going to a computer display at your local library, joining a house tour, learning to tango, volunteering at a hospital, signing up for a pet grooming course. Review your clippings once a month.

4.   Practice makes playtime. Here's a start. Rethink the word "errand." Find a private sanctuary no more than ten minutes away from your home or office. Tell yourself and others that you're heading to the dry cleaners or drugstore and escape to one of these peaceful haunts. Quiet is the key here. No cell phones allowed.

5.   If your practice went well, guess what? You get to pass "Go," which means meditating with your calendar open. How does the next month look? Which day could you take off without your world grinding to a halt? Write down "Soul Care" on that date. Now you have eight hours to call your own. Play hooky, baby. Misbehave, sweetie darling. Do what you want to do, not what has to be done.

What did you do? How did it feel? Good enough to try again? Block out another day in the next three months—something to really look forward to.

Write Your Way into Wholeness

You Are Allowed to Color Outside the Lines

When we are writing, or painting, or composing, we are, during the time of creativity, freed from normal restrictions, and are opened to a wider world, where colors are brighter, sounds clearer and people are more wondrously complex than we normally realize.

Madeleine L'Engle

Chapter 9

Learning to Let Go

One knows what one has lost,
but not what one may find.

GEORGE SAND

Are you open to Life's spontaneous gifts—or have your expectations of what you wanted kept you from seeing Life's generosity?

What did you want to do last year that hasn't happened yet? Perhaps you'd intended to paint your house or refinish the floors in your kitchen. Maybe you'd hoped to take a bicycle trip or learn to play tennis—or just spend the day at a great flea market or auction.

Now think about the things that have happened that you didn't expect. A wonderful visit from an old friend or family member. A swimming prize for your child. Beautiful blush-pink roses in your garden; no deadly raids from deer or mites. Maybe you made a new friend at the office annual picnic, when you thought you'd know everyone who would be there.

Serendipity is the happy surprise that comes from the unexpected. What serendipitous events have graced your life in the last few months?

Sarah Ban Breathnach

Today, just try slowing down. Approach the day as if it were an adagio— a melody played in an easy, graceful manner. Listen to music that soothes and uplifts your spirit. And while you listen, pause to consider how all the individual notes come together harmoniously to give expression to the entire score.

SIMPLE ABUNDANCE
JANUARY 17

I remember so well when I first realized I was depriving myself of pleasure by expecting things always to go exactly my way. The epiphany came the day of a dinner party I'd been planning. First thing that morning, I set out for our local farmer's market, picturing in my mind the delicious ratatouille I would prepare. But at the market I couldn't find what I wanted: both the eggplant and the zucchini looked wilted and beat-up.

Feeling cross, I was forced to abandon my shopping list and take another look around. When I did I saw fresh lettuces, mushrooms, goat cheese, watercress, scrumptious flame-red and yellow tomatoes, herbs, crisp radishes, crusty loaves of newly baked bread. I realized that all the makings of a wonderfully fresh salad extravaganza were right there in front of me. Even now, years later, my friends rave about the meal I served that night.

Have you ever been praised for or felt proud of something you did that came not from laborious planning or efforts but from rolling with the punches, rising to the occasion, seizing a moment or opportunity, or "making lemonade from lemons"? Describe your unexpected triumph here:

It took this chance triumph to make me realize how my focus on a rigid list of mental expectations had blinded me to happy surprises. This limiting mindscape didn't apply just to my menu preparation, but also to my work, intimate relationships, even my behavior as a parent. For example, if my daughter didn't show the enthusiasm I expected after a carefully orchestrated birthday party, I would get annoyed—and feel compelled to ask her, "So did you have fun?" Or if I'd planned a girls' night out with a friend and she had to cancel at the last minute, I would allow my sense of letdown to escalate into a feeling of being slighted—after all, I'd moved Heaven and earth for us to get together, and she hadn't.

I was, in other words, a hard-core expectator. And yet I was always perplexed as to why I was so unhappy when I had so many reasons to give thanks.

When was the last time you let yourself be dragged down by expecting a certain outcome to a situation, and not receiving it? Describe one such moment here. How could you have found pleasure or joy in that event in place of disappointment?

Holding on to expectations is a pretty feeble way to try to control our lives. It limits us in more ways than we know. An old neighbor or a beloved colleague moves away, and your sense of loss prevents you from being open to the new person who moves in. Even though you dropped broad hints, your husband fails to buy you a nightgown for your anniversary—and your disappointment prevents you from appreciating the sweater he picked out instead.

We need to see life as it is, not to hold ourselves captive to a vision of how it ought to be. We need to let go of our incessant need to impose order, except in our own household and work habits. We need to make space in our days and plans so that new things can enter our lives. Surrendering expectations opens us up for the gifts of spontaneity, serendipity, and serenity, enabling us to cast off old agendas of what's supposed to make us happy. However, this has been one of my hardest life lessons. And yet when I do, I am always amazed at how life surprises me with joy.

You will be too.

The Loves That Got Away

We love because it is the only true adventure.

NIKKI GIOVANNI

We all have our favorite ways to mark the magic of life's current romances—the people, places, and pleasures—that fill our daily round with meaning and color our dreams for the future with a rosy hue. But sometimes glimpsing an old photo or dusting a sentimental object can evoke sorrow disguised as wistfulness. In only a few seconds your heart is racing again, trapped in an old cycle of pain or even ancient rage, as memory reassigns blame and reinforces guilt. I know a woman who has been known to burst into tears in an elevator when she hears a piped-in rendition of *their song,* going back twenty-five years and two marriages.

These melancholy murmurs can be devastating. I used to dismiss them as fast as I could, and I suspect that I'm not alone. We turn our hearts away from what feels like a horrific accumulation of wrecked dreams and failed efforts, afraid that whatever killed our old love is poised waiting to strike again. And we bury or discard anything that might trigger feelings of loss. I have one friend who threw out not only all her personal mementos accumulated during a disastrous love affair, but even the professional awards she received during that period, just to make sure there's nothing to remind her of that former pain. Another friend gave away every item of clothing she owned after she divorced, as if even her favorite blouse had become contaminated with traces of bad luck.

But when we run and hide, we see our world through a filter of fear and self-loathing. We assume that both the love and the loss were not only some terrible mistake but that it was all our fault, *our fault alone.* If the relationship was lonely and unfulfilling, it must have been because of something we did or said or didn't say or do. After a particularly bittersweet love affair (made all the more bitter because of the occasional sweetness), I seriously questioned every choice I had made during the tumultuous year I had been with this man, convinced that if I'd been so wrong about a man, I must have been wrong about everything else too. In my attempts to renounce anything even remotely associated with the source of my sorrow, I stopped going to favorite haunts and hanging out with mutual friends, moved from an apartment I adored and seriously considered changing my professional path simply because my former boyfriend shared it. Thank God I didn't, because while this man wasn't the love of my life, he did ignite my passion for the written word that became my life's love.

So how do you change your perspective on abandonment and loss? Look for their hidden gifts. Why do you still wear red on your most important occasions? Because once upon a time you were his gorgeous lady in red. Why do you speak Italian? Because it was his native language, and he helped you to learn it. Discovering the hidden gifts enables you to ransom back the discarded remnants of yourself. But in order to do this you must revisit the loves of your life and search for the good in each past relationship until you find it.

I know this sounds scary, and, if the loss is a recent one, perhaps impossible. But with the hindsight of even a year, it can be reassuring and healing to acknowledge all the good your past loves gave you. We cannot let go of a person or situation that caused us pain until we're willing to bless it, and we can't do that until we find something worth blessing.

When glancing back, stop assuming that all your past actions and emotions were wrong; from this moment on assume that they were right. There were precious reasons you were drawn to your former loves, but also positive ones for moving on.

Look deeply. Don't be fooled by superficial explanations. Perhaps you shouldn't have been so understanding of his needs to the exclusion of your own, but now at least you know what your needs are. Instead of thinking you are a quitter for giving up the piano in favor of taking up one of his hobbies, or a loser for blindly following him to a strange city, admit that playing piano never suited you anyway, and that the city he brought you to is the one you now live in happily and have learned to love, even without him.

I'd be lying if I said that if I could live my life all over again, I'd do it exactly the same way. But I wouldn't wish away a single past love despite moments of darkness and despair I thought I'd never survive. Great grief is only born out of great joy, and our anguish is that we feel we shall never, ever love as truly, as madly, or as deeply again.

The English poet Elizabeth Barrett Browning believed that her husband, the poet Robert Browning, whom she married when she was forty, had "loved her into full being." For most of my life I thought that this wonderful sense of completion was only found in Love's reciprocal promise. But now I wonder if Loss wasn't also an attentive suitor to my soul? Why? Because it was only during the lonely and bereft times that I have learned how to love myself into Wholeness.

So be willing to look back with gratitude at the loves left behind. If you can, you'll discover that all you thought to be lost and lacking is really waiting to be found and cherished within you.

Before Change Comes

Everything in life that we really accept undergoes a change.

KATHERINE MANSFIELD

Before you can change anything in your life you have to accept your current situation. And you can't accept it until you know what it is—the truth of the situation. Sometimes it takes a long time to uncover the truth. It's all a process—tiny, tiny steps.

I think of acceptance as the long sigh of the soul. It's when you say, "Okay, this is what's happening now. But things will be okay."

"Acceptance of what has happened is the first step in overcoming the consequence of any misfortune," the philosopher William James tells us. Is there an "If only . . . " holding you back today? What is it? Has the reality of what or how your life is today become easier to live with, or harder because of those two words? Are you willing to let them go from your vocabulary?

A friend lost his daughter in an automobile accident, and for months he was in deep mourning. There was little any of us could do to comfort him. But one thing he said after some time passed struck me. "You get to the point where you realize you have to stop saying 'If only,' he told me. 'If only she hadn't been in that car, if only I had made her stay home that day. If only she had left an hour later . . . '"

He began to find some measure of comfort. He was able to climb out of the abyss when he stopped saying "If only," ceased fighting against what had happened, and began to accept it.

Acceptance is surrendering to what is: our circumstances, our feelings, our problems, our financial status, our work, our health, our relationships. I have learned that when I surrender to the reality of a particular situation—when I don't continue to resist, but accept—a softening in my soul occurs. Suddenly I am able to open up to receive all the goodness and abundance available to me because acceptance brings with it so much relief and release.

When we let go, when we relax into the reality of our lives, people can approach us. When a friend retired, she told me that people suddenly began speaking to her in shops because she lingered rather than rushed. Without her awareness, she was signaling that she was open. She was letting go of the isolation of busyness.

Describe a time in your life when surrendering to reality made it surprisingly easier to handle a tough situation:

Declare out loud to the Universe that you are willing to let go of struggle and eager to learn through joy. It just may take you at your word. What's more, you'll discover, much to your amazement and delight, that such blessings have been waiting patiently for you to claim them all along.

SIMPLE ABUNDANCE
JANUARY 19

Secret Anniversaries

*How we remember, what we remember,
and why we remember form the most
personal map of our individuality.*

CHRISTINA BALDWIN

The poet Henry Wadsworth Longfellow believed that the "holiest of all holidays" are not the ones on our calendars, but the ones we observe "in silence and apart." He called these special days our "secret anniversaries of the heart."

Secret anniversaries often reveal, in mystical ways, our place in the world and our relationship to ourselves and others. They can be joyful or sad, major turning points or minor epiphanies. You might remember the day you got a coveted part in the school play or received a special love letter or sent your child off for his first sleepover. Or you might recall a painful loss: the due date of a baby who was never born, the day an adored parent passed away. Sometimes, it takes long years to recognize the importance of such a secret anniversary— or to even know that you have one calling to be commemorated.

We all have secret anniversaries of the heart. They may be major life events like the death of a loved one, or an instance that would seem almost frivolous to someone else, but has particular resonance for us. What are some of your secret anniversaries of the heart? How did you honor one?

Our senses are the conduits of these sacred soul memories, the pathways that can lead to powerful revelations. What is your favorite scent? Something wonderful simmering on the stove? The fragrance of newly mown grass? A wood fire? Suntan lotion? For me, there's something about a hot summer afternoon and the smell of a barn—warm leather, sweat, hay, and horses—that transports me to my past.

What are your favorite scents, the ones that short-circuit the passage of time for you? Follow your nose to the memory of a profound passage that is probably deeply buried. Describe the fragrance of memory:

Sometimes we dismiss these tugs of remembrance as sentimental or unimportant. But honoring the personal passages that alter the trajectory of our lives is how we grow and change and heal—and find the strength to continue on our mysterious journey to Wholeness. Agatha Christie believed that "one's memories represent those moments which, insignificant as they may seem, never the less represent the inner self and one-self as most really oneself." The past asks only to be acknowledged.

Banish Perfectionism

In order to go on living one must try to escape the death involved in perfection.

HANNAH ARENDT

We are all so hard on ourselves. I am no longer quite so bad about this, but there was a time when I wanted everything in my life to be perfect. If I was having company for dinner I would spend hours setting the table, and if my daughter walked in and wanted to help me, perhaps by folding the napkins, I would refold those napkins after she left because they weren't perfect. Now if I'm setting the table and my daughter volunteers to help, thank God I know that the most beautiful sight in that room is her face. The napkins will become soiled, the guests will leave. All that matters is the perfection of love.

When you cut and paste magazine pictures into your Illustrated Discovery Journal, please remember that the settings in most of those scenes you've chosen are *illusion.* Monthly, glossy, airbrushed visions of the unattainable. These pictures are not meant for us to imitate, because we can't. They're just meant to inspire us. We can't achieve that perfection and shouldn't try to. God knows, as do the magazine editors, that it took a dozen experts to carefully craft the source of our sorrow.

Leaf through a magazine and choose a picture that represents your ideal room. It'll never happen in your lifetime, right? Now look closely at it. What in the photo has any relation to your own home? Is the sofa the same shape? Is the clock on the wall like the one you inherited from your favorite aunt? Where's the connection to *your* reality? Can you find the possible in the seemingly improbable? How can you reject the "perfect" and find happiness in flashes of the attainable? Life becomes sublime when we seek reality perfected, not perfection.

Perfection does not exist on this physical plane. I don't even think Spirit sought perfection in Heaven because it leaves such little room for improvement. I am always comforted by the realization that after the seventh day of creation, God didn't say, "And it's perfect." Spirit declared, *It is very good.* And that's good enough for me. How about you?

Perfectionism is a disease of low self-esteem. Like workaholism, perfectionism is a version of self-loathing. When we were young, nothing we ever did was good enough, so we just kept on doing until doing was all we could do. When doing more and more didn't make a difference, we wondered if perhaps doing our work perfectly would make the mark. When we got all A's, suddenly voices other than our own sang our praises and for one minute we rested. But when the praise stopped we committed to setting in motion a cycle of self-destruction instigated by the silence of others.

When have you worked and worked at something, purely for the praise it brought you from others? How did that feel? How could you change your behavior to reflect self-congratulation and pride instead of focusing on and needing the admiration of others?

You can see how we're dealing not only with what the world tells us we should be, we're dealing with our own very deep-rooted belief that we're not good enough. But when you discover who you really are, you realize that being your glorious self is better than being good enough.

What I did to try to break the perfectionist habit (and one never becomes cured, one is always recovering . . .) was to get a little egg timer with sand in it, and I recommend you do the same. As part of my meditative practice in the morning, I would turn the egg timer over and just watch the grains of sand disappear. It was a powerful reminder that time is finite, and each morning I'd ask myself how I wanted to be spending it. How much of your life is frittered away by the neurotic insistence on perfection? Learning to let go means leaving

We no longer have the luxury of wallowing in what's held us back; this is the emotional baggage we're supposed to be getting rid of this time around.

SOMETHING MORE
"THE SACRED
ADVENTURE"

188

space in our life, work, attitude, and expectations for the subtle nuances of Spirit. On any day's blank canvas try mastering the broad strokes, and life's mystical fine lines will appear where they are supposed to be.

Letting Go of the Ultimate Seductor

When I'm trusting and being myself as fully
as possible, everything in my life reflects this
by falling into place easily, often miraculously.

SHAKTI GAWAIN

Our work, especially if it's our grand passion, can be so seductive that we can find ourselves completely caught up in its rapture, unable to resist. But the ultimate seduction is often accompanied by the ultimate addictions: workaholism and perfectionism. What makes these two reckless behavior patterns so dangerous is that they're sanctioned, supported and sustained by a society still shackled to the Puritan work ethic. The Puritans frowned on anything enjoyable, believing that God's favor could be achieved only by grueling struggle, stringent self-discipline, and backbreaking work. But Spirit can't use us to heal the world if we can't heal ourselves.

I love Virginia Woolf's warning about workaholism. "If people are highly successful in their professions, they lose their senses. Sight goes. They have no time to look at pictures. Sound goes. They have no time to listen to music. Speech goes. They have no time for conversation. They lose their sense of proportion—the relations between one thing and another. Humanity goes."

When we succumb to workaholism, what's really happening is that we have lost faith in Spirit's willingness to help us achieve success. Asking for grace doesn't seem as practical as working round the clock.

When was the last time Spirit accompanied you to work?

When was the last time you asked It to?

Quietly scrutinize your working cycle. Try to make it more in harmony with your own rhythms. Start small. Think baby steps. How would you define it currently? Do you try to do many things at once? Or do you focus on one task at a time? Do you do your hardest work in the morning, when you are freshest, or later in the day when you feel that you're in a groove? Look at one week of your life and make a timeline for each day, recording the periods of work, play, exercise, thought, etc. Do you see any patterns? Do you notice that you've filled time with activities that are neither necessary to your daily life nor fulfilling to you? List five things you'd like to change about the way you use your time each day:

Working from home is becoming an attractive economic alternative as women try to bring more harmony into their daily round. Many women are leaving the downsized corporate world to start home-based businesses.

But if you're not careful, it's very easy to blur the distinction between the two spheres, home and work. Once you realize how comfortable, even pleasurable, it can be to work at home, it's easy to become ruthless, taking on more than you can handle reasonably. Since you don't have a commute, you can start an hour earlier and continue an hour later, and weekends are perfect for "catching up."

And if your entire home turns into an office, how do you have space to let others in? Or yourself to live?

Even if you're earning more money than you did before, if you no longer have a life at home you must learn to set limits.

Working from home can be a genuine step toward self-determination, once we honor the sense of balance we originally sought before we left the traditional office setup.

Maybe you haven't burned out yet, but the time has come for change. Consider your ideal working day. If you could work in any style or setting, what would it be? What are your ideal working hours? Imagine your ideal workplace surroundings. What do you see?

Now compare the ideal with the real. Is there any common ground? Can you introduce one ideal element into your present working environment? All of us can begin working with what we've got.

Chapter 9 — Moodlings

Learning to Let Go

1. List three objects you own, songs you hear, or places you return to—like the restaurant where you had a special meal, the song that played during your first kiss—that can still send you into an emotional tizzy after all these years.

2. Now look again at the list above. What happy, warm memories surface, triggered by those same items? What positive and immeasurable difference to your life has remained with you because of that experience (even if it's only a lesson about what *not* to do next time!).

3. Nothing that once made us feel happy and fulfilled is ever lost. There is a golden thread that runs through each of our lives. We just need to rediscover this thread. What is your golden thread, the thread that links the major events of your life? Go back and reconstruct your personal narrative of major events from the perspective that each had a positive effect on the outcome of your life.

4. Here's a therapeutic exercise: Write down a series of "what ifs"—stretch back into your memory to come up with as many as you can. Read over this list. Now crumple it into a ball and pitch it. You've truly gotten rid of them now, so revel in the closure this brings.

5.   What's your favorite season? Why? In what ways can you *go with* each season, enjoying its fruits, its attributes—instead of fighting against it? In Europe, good cooks know that the best meals are made up of the foods that nature is presenting right then—no waxy, colorless tomatoes in winter for them! How can you bring the lushest, most flavorful, rich, colorful moments to your life?

6.   If there is one problem, regret, sorrow, or loss you could let go of right now, what would it be?

Would you like help? Okay. Write the source of your misery on a piece of paper. Be specific in your detail. Who, what, how, where. Now burn the past in a large fireproof container. Scatter the ashes to the wind. Breathe a sigh of relief. Give thanks. Go on.

Write Your Way into Wholeness

You Can Never Go Back, but You Won't Want to Anyway

I fling my past behind me like a robe
Worn threadbare in the seams, and out of date.
I have outgrown it.

                        Ella Wheeler Wilcox

Chapter 10

Sacred Connections

Intimate relationships cannot
substitute for a life plan.

HARRIET LERNER

Many of us settle for something less than love, even in our most intimate relationships," the contemporary spiritual writer and poet Kathleen Norris admits, surely for us all, in her exquisite book *Amazing Grace: A Vocabulary of Faith.* "Most of us know couples who despise each other and yet stay together, living as if in an armed camp."

The truth is, our marriages are only as emotionally healthy, happy, holy, and content as we are. We can divorce a man, but we can't divorce ourselves; we learn the truth about ourselves through our personal relationships.

"When we bury feelings, we also bury ourselves," Nathaniel Branden tells us in *The Psychology of Self-Esteem.* "It means we exist in a state of alienation. We rarely know it, but we are lonely for ourselves."

Who are you lonely for tonight? Do you know? The writer Mary Renault believed that "All tragedies deal with fated meetings. . . . Fate deals its stroke; sorrow is purged, or turned to rejoicing; there is death, or triumph; there has been a meeting, and a change. No one will ever make a tragedy—and that is as well, for one

197

could not bear it—whose grief is that the principals never met."

And yet countless women bear this grief every day because we have not met the One we came to this earth to be reunited with—our Authentic Self.

"Many women today feel a sadness we cannot name. Though we accomplish much of what we set out to do, we sense that something is missing in our lives and—fruitlessly—search out there for the answers," the writer Emily Hancock points out. "What's often wrong is that we are disconnected from an authentic sense of self."

You've Got Mail

Nothing exists unless it is on paper.

ANAÏS NIN

You know that you have really reached the end of the relationship as soon as you stop looking to see if he's sent e-mail. Likewise, as soon as lust starts rearranging your heartbeat patterns, you know that you are embarking on an affair to remember, at least from your end. "Before words, there is, of course, desire. Language is the thread joining that desire to its object, explaining its needs, expressing its cries," the writer Michelle Lovric tells us. "The love letter is our heart on our sleeve, our battle standard, our essence, our indelible signature, our emotional fingerprint, our private well of memory, our own ghost of kisses past, our true secret self."

Having been born an incurable romantic, I have been writing love letters—to my father, my kindergarten teacher, Tommy Maher down the block, ever since I was able to put crayon to paper. The story of most women's lives is written in X's and O's. Michelle Lovric, editor of two anthologies of famous love letters as well as her own delicious primer, *How to Write Love Letters,* unravels the mystery of this clandestine compulsion. "We write letters because they last, even when the love that inspired them has gone, leaving little other trace. . . . We write letters because we are all insecure. We cannot hear often enough that we are loved. . . . We can scarcely believe our luck. . . . Writing love letters are graceful palliatives for the lonely, the lustful, the needy and the disbelieving."

We also write love letters because words are potent go-betweens, able to successfully woo potential lovers far more persuasively, we believe, than we ever could in person. I mean, just look at us. Do you remember the story of Cyrano de Bergerac, the gallant sixteenth-century French poet and swordsman, who is asked by a young soldier in his regiment to help him seduce the woman he adores, Roxanne, by ghost-writing his love letters? The only problem is that Cyrano also loves Roxanne. However, since he is so grotesquely ugly, rejection is all he has ever known and so he conceals his feelings. But when Cyrano's pen caresses Roxanne on paper

Today make getting in touch with the Silence within yourself your first priority. As you do, you will be amazed at how everything else seems to find its own order.

SIMPLE ABUNDANCE
FEBRUARY 25

on his friend's behalf, de Bergerac's passion for her can no longer be restrained. Naturally, Roxanne falls deeply in love with her rapturous correspondent, believing him to be the handsome soldier who stands beneath her balcony each night. Eventually she learns the true identities of both men and chooses Cyrano because the beauty of his soul and the depth of his passion eclipse his physical limitations. In love's eyes he is beautiful, and she feels blessed to have found such a man.

There is a little Cyrano in every love letter writer. In a letter we can be bold and still hide. My first serious romantic correspondence was when I was a sophomore in high school and a girlfriend fixed me up with a midshipman at the U.S. Naval Academy. But the date for the big dance was several months away and so we began a correspondence. Mail call was a much anticipated event each day and my witty, clever, and heartfelt paper arrows always hit the target. I know this because when we broke up, he told me he would miss my letters. I hope he did.

Since there would be many versions before an actual letter was sent, early on I got into the habit of keeping my rough drafts. I knew that what I was mining here was pure gold. Writing love letters to others led me to somewhere I could have never found on my own—the depths of my soul. Because I got and gave so much joy from these letters, they have always been my favorite form of writing. When I began my own excavation process I rediscovered decades of these letters, the paper ruins of each romance neatly bundled in a different colored ribbon.

As I slowly began to reread them, I made a startling discovery. If I paid no attention to whom a particular letter was sent, I really couldn't tell one beau from another; in fact, a few times I didn't have a clue because most of my letters began with the very handy *Dearest and Best*. . . . But the voice of the woman was the same—intense, passionate, funny, and dramatic. I would laugh as I reread these letters, I would cry, I would sigh. I was held enthralled by the writer's ability to weave a spell as she seduced the reader into loving her. It didn't matter who the reader actually was.

More often than it feels comfortable to admit, I would also cringe to think that I'd written something so breathtaking to such a moron. And then the epiphany occurred. It didn't matter how old I was, where I was, or to whom the envelope was addressed. *I wasn't writing these letters to a man, I was writing them to myself.* The heart, soul, and mind I was seeking to seduce was my own. My whole life I'd been the object of desire, and I had never realized it.

The truth does set you free.

Now I want you to try a little experiment. Who does your heart desire right now? Who do you secretly swoon over? Get *Dearest and Best* in your mind's eye, no matter how silly or far-fetched it seems. Now I want you to write the most fabulous, passionate love letter you can imagine to this person but the salutation should begin, *My darling, Sweetheart, My own, Deeply beloved*. . . . (To prime your inspiration peruse Michelle Lovric's glorious books, *Love Letters: An Anthology of Passion, Pas-*

sionate Love Letters: An Anthology of Desire, and *How to Write Love Letters.*) When you come up for air, let it rip. After you're done, put the letter in an envelope and address it to yourself. Wait a week. Now mail it. When it arrives, open it slowly and let the thrill of the words wash over you. How does it make you feel? Warm? Tingly? Loved? Good. This is very good. Woman was created to be adored.

For once you have been worshipped and appreciated as you so richly deserve. Trust me, life and love are completely different from this point on. As Oscar Wilde so wonderfully put it, "To love oneself is the beginning of a lifelong romance."

Changing Relationships

People change and forget to tell each other.

LILLIAN HELLMAN

When you change—and it may take you several years to change, though it's going to feel like the speed of light—your relationships with everyone are going to change too. Not only with your partner, but with your children, your friends, your parents, your colleagues. You may feel alone, but we do not live isolated lives. Suddenly you're not available to do

Deliberately seeking solitude—quality time spent away from family and friends— may seem selfish. It is not. Solitude is as necessary for our creative spirits to develop and flourish as are sleep and food for our bodies to survive.

SIMPLE ABUNDANCE
JULY 22

the things people have expected you to do and that you've been doing for the past ten or twenty or thirty years. And because they feel threatened, you're going to get questions that make both parties feel uncomfortable. Gradual change is how you gently push past your own and other people's comfort zones.

The most emotionally charged area of change—be it positive or negative—will be in your intimate personal relationships. So let time be your ally. You don't emerge one morning after having gone to bed the night before and say, "Enough! There are going to be some changes around here!" But it might seem that way to others.

In her book *Intimate Partners: Patterns in Love and Marriage,* Maggie Scarf describes how when couples come together they usually have unconsciously agreed upon the amount of intimacy and autonomy they want in their relationship. They both want the same balance and boundaries. So when one partner begins to change, pulling away or drawing closer, the implicit agreement shifts. Inevitably the other partner will react, often trying to maintain the same degree of intimacy and autonomy as they had before. But if new terms can be agreed on, the results can be very exciting.

"I don't think marriages break up because of what you do to each other," Carol Matthau tells us. "They break up because of what you must become in order to stay in them."

When a relationship is lonely and unfulfilling, you

can begin to shut down until you feel you are disappearing. "How much of my true self I camouflage and choke in order to commend myself to him, denying the fullness of me," Sylvia Ashton-Warner wrote in 1943. "How I've toned myself down, diluted myself to maintain his approval."

That's why every woman must at some point in her life become courageous enough to turn away from the prism of her relationships as the reflector of her worth.

Describe the first time that people started noticing a change in you. What did they say, how did you respond?

When was the last time you felt as if you shut down so that you could keep someone else's approval?

Second-Guessing Spirit

*I think there is no suffering greater
than what is caused by the doubts of
those who want to believe.*

FLANNERY O'CONNOR

The nineteenth-century Danish philosopher Søren Kierkegaard said that any act of creation is like the process of pregnancy. For the first three months especially, you have to think of the creative conception as if it were a fetus and you were protecting it in the same way a mother protects a child. You must do the same thing on this path. Don't announce to the world, "I'm going to find my Authentic Self. I'm going to start living the life for which I was born." Instead think of yourself as a member of the French underground. You need to protect yourself, because many dreams have been derailed by other people's advice offered "for your own good."

"You're too old." "You don't have the resources." "You haven't finished your college education." "Who will take care of the kids?" "It could take you ten years to do it." "It's been done before." "You don't have the money."

Be careful about confiding your sacred dreams, especially in this period that Kierkegaard called "dreaming consciousness."

Second thoughts have aborted more dreams than

all the difficult circumstances, overwhelming obstacles, and dangerous detours fate could ever throw at you. Undermining your authenticity by succumbing to someone's negative opinion is a subtle form of self-abuse. Few of us are immune to the opinions of others.

Don't confide your dreams to people who have told you all your life that you can't do things. If you suspect you know the answer you're going to hear, why bother asking this person for their advice? Instead, find somebody whose mind is open to the positive possibilities of new choice and chance.

A short-story writer I know used to take fiction-writing courses with a great teacher at Columbia University. The teacher would urge her students not to tell anyone about their ideas—they should simply begin writing, and suspending their critical faculties as they did so (later, in subsequent drafts, they could read with a critical eye). "That which is clamoring for expression inside you doesn't care how it comes out," the instructor would say. "So save it for your work, let it find its way. Don't confide it early and let others stop you."

This applies not only to writing but to living. So don't share the process you're going through until you're well into it, until the positive changes in you bloom outwardly. Maybe you're smiling more now, or you seem more relaxed. Whatever the outward signs, it is only when others start commenting and complementing that you know the time has come to share your secret.

Write down some of the reactions you've gotten

When we are finally willing to relinquish the need to live through others and acknowledge that we deserve a life of our own choosing, we are ready to move on and be born again through the reembodiment journey.

SOMETHING MORE
"YOUR OWN
NATURAL SELECTION
PROCESS"

from others as you've been on the Simple Abundance path. (Be sure to note who made each comment):

Around this time, you're also going to start noticing that there are some friends who lift you up and always carry you along, just as you carry them. And then there are others who are very negative and their negativity pulls you down, even though you love them and have loved them for years. But as you grow into your authenticity, as you reclaim your own life, you will find in yourself the courage to disengage from the toxic relationships that have stifled you and cause you pain.

Carl Jung said, "The meeting of two personalities is like the contract of two chemical substances: if there is any reaction, both are transformed."

What transformative relationships do you cherish? Why? How has your friendship transformed another?

"The real mirror of your life and soul is your true friend," John O'Donohue reminds us. "A friend helps you to glimpse who you really are and what you are doing here."

Who are your soul friends, the people with whom you truly belong and feel safe? The ones with whom you feel that your Authentic Self can emerge, be appreciated and loved?

How do you define a good relationship?

"Friends are people who help you be more yourself," Merle Shain reminds us, "more the person you are intended to be."

Who has helped you become more yourself?

Who loves you unconditionally? Who can you call at 3 A.M.? Who would bail you out of jail and not ask questions?

Chapter 10 — Moodlings

Sacred Connections

1.   I believe that none of us has any idea of the countless lives we touch and change for the better in the course of our lifetime. Think of the dozens of people whose lives you have affected, recently and long ago, and how a small kindness of yours has made a difference. To whom have you brought joy and meaning, in large or small ways?

2.   There is only one you. Your unique impact on the lives of your friends, family, neighbors and coworkers is a special gift. If you had to auction off this rare quality that makes you uniquely you, how would you describe your special gift in the auction catalog?

3.   When was the first time you realized you wanted to make a significant change in your life? How did you feel? Uneasy? Thrilled? Scared? Overwhelmed? Did you make the change? Was it worth it?

4.   Have you ever bought greeting cards for yourself, just because they strike you as funny, or as particularly suited to you? No holiday this week? Celebrate yourself by writing a message in a card, just from you, to you.

Write Your Way into Wholeness

Wooing the Love That Dare Not Speak Your Name

When something so vital has been abused for so long, it is sometimes hard to coax it back. By seeking out our souls, honouring them, and allowing the passion to reinhabit them, we enable the discovery of our authentic selves.

Caitlin Matthews

Chapter 11

Authentic Success

Dwells within the soul of every Artist
More that all [her] efforts can express
And [she] knows the best remains unuttered,
Sighing at what we call [her] success.

ADELAIDE ANNE PROCTER

Authentic success is different for each one of us. No single definition fits all women because we come in different sizes.

Perhaps these words will sound familiar to you, but I have never been able to define authentic success more clearly than this, and frequently I need to be reminded exactly what it is that I am pursuing every day. Authentic success is having time enough to enjoy personal pursuits that bring you pleasure, time enough to bestow loving gestures upon your family, time enough to care for your home, tend your garden, nurture your soul. It means never having to tell yourself or those you love, "Maybe next year." Knowing that if today were your last day on earth, you could leave without regret. Feeling focused and serene when you work, not fragmented. It's knowing that you've done the best that you possibly can,

Sarah Ban Breathnach

For each of us there is a deeply personal dream waiting to be discovered and fulfilled. When we cherish our dream and then invest love, creative energy, perseverance, and passion in ourselves, we will achieve an authentic success.

SIMPLE ABUNDANCE
JANUARY 20

no matter what circumstances you faced; it's knowing in your soul that the best you can do is *all* you can do, and that the best you can do is always enough.

Authentic success is knowing there is a difference between a job and vocation. "Vocation" comes from the Latin *vocare,* "to call." We have all had jobs, and we all have a calling.

Authentic success is knowing that true contentment comes from being adept at change, because life is change.

Authentic success is accepting your limitations, making peace with your past, and reveling in your passions so that your future may unfold according to a Divine Plan. Authentic success is knowing that there is a Divine Plan for your life and it's meant to make you happy. It's discovering and calling forth your gifts and offering them to the world to help heal its ravaged heart.

Authentic success is not just money in the bank but a contented heart and peace of mind. It's earning what you feel you deserve for the work you do and knowing that you're worth it. Authentic success is paying your bills with ease, taking care of all your needs and the needs of those you love, indulging some wants, and having enough left over to save and share.

Authentic success is not about accumulating but about letting go, because all you have is all you truly need. It is feeling good about who you are, appreciating where you've been, celebrating your achievements, and honoring the distance you've already come. Authentic success is reaching the point where *being* is as impor-

tant as *doing*. It is the steady pursuit of a dream. It's realizing that no matter how much time it takes for a dream
to come true in the physical world, no day is ever wasted.
It's valuing inner as well as outer labor—both yours and
others'. It is elevating labor to a craft and craft to an art
by bringing Love to every task you undertake.

Authentic success is knowing how simply abun-
dant your life is exactly as it is today. It is being so grateful for the many blessings bestowed on you and yours
that you can share your portion with others. One workshop participant told us that on the day she received a
prize promotion at work, she glowed with happiness;
she wanted *everyone* to be able to have what they want.

Living authentic success means trusting your instincts; when to expand and withdraw. Michael Jordan
knew. Anna Quindlen knew when to switch from writing newspaper columns to writing novels, and when to
return to the newspaper column. Her choice wasn't
about career versus family, it was about worldly success
versus authentic success; she honored her heart.

Only the heart knows what is working in our lives.
When you listen to your heart and follow its wisdom,
you've achieved authentic success, because authentic
success is living each day with a heart overflowing with
gratitude.

Authentic Success in Work

To love what you do and feel that it matters—
how could anything be more fun.

KATHARINE GRAHAM

Sometimes we are recognized not for what we think will bring us glory, but for something else. Benvenuto Cellini, the Renaissance sculptor, believed himself a genius as an artist and wrote an autobiography recording his achievements. Today he is best known not for his artworks but for the autobiography that conveys the spirit of his age, but he didn't consider it significant.

Each of us was created to give outward expression to Divinity through our personal gifts. Sharing our gifts with the world is our Great Work, no matter what our job description might be or how our résumé reads.

"No matter what we do, we can make it our ministry," Marianne Williamson writes in her illuminating *A Return to Love: Reflections on the Principles of a Course in Miracles.* "No matter what form our job or activity takes, the content is the same as everyone else's; we are here to minister to human hearts. If we talk to anyone, or see anyone, or even think of anyone, then we have the opportunity to bring more love into the universe . . . there is no one whose job is unimportant to God."

Why is the axiom "Do what you love and the money will follow" true? Because doing what you love is not about money, it's about wonder. As soon as you understand that you're supposed to be asking for wonder in your work instead of money, you'll start experiencing abundance.

Achieving Financial Serenity

To me, money is alive. It's almost human. If you treat it with real sympathy and kindness and consideration, it will be a good servant and work hard for you, and stay with you and take care of you. If you treat it arrogantly and contemptuously, as if it were not human, as if it were only a slave and could work without limit, it will turn on you with a great revenge and leave you to look after yourself alone.

KATHARINE BUTLER HATHAWAY

Like success, money is an emotionally volatile issue. It's probably the most complicated relationship we have—and the one that most controls our lives because we let it.

"People are funny about money," says a very rich businesswoman who has seen her personal relationships fall apart over it. "It took me a long time to realize the side effects of wealth and how it can change people," she said.

Jacob Needleman, in his book *Money and the Meaning of Life,* tells us that money influences every aspect of our lives: "The money factor is there, wrapped around or lodged inside everything. Think of what you want or

Transforming every "What will I do?" into "What can I do?" fuels your fiscal creativity, restoring a sense of peace as you pursue prosperity.

SIMPLE ABUNDANCE
OCTOBER 24

what you dream of, for now, or next year, or for the rest of your life. It will take money, a certain, definite amount."

We are hypocritical about money. We want it, but we don't want to appear as if we do; we fear and desire it in the same heartbeat. Professor Needleman believes that money is a force we must face today in much the same way sex was an issue for previous generations. What is undeniable is that money is the raw material from which we build our lives.

But we confuse spiritual yearnings with material wants. We long for serenity. But in becoming experts at quantity instead of quality, we rob our souls of Real Life's richness.

In order to find balance between the two spheres that pull us in opposite directions—material and spiritual—Needleman suggests we consider the practical advice in the ancient admonishment: "Render unto Caesar that which is Caesar's and unto God that which is God's." A modern translation of this might be: Give as much of your time, creative energy, and emotion to the world as is necessary to sustain your body, but keep your heart for yourself and your soul for Spirit.

However, this requires essential information, understanding "what in ourselves belongs to the transcendent realm and what to the material realm. And then to give to each what is due to each."

Worrying about money repels rather than attracts prosperity. This worry sends toxic signals: fear, lack, deprivation. When your subconscious mind continually

Affirming our abundance now, by becoming generous givers, dramatically demonstrates our prosperity to the doubter within. Let your authentic self convince her and watch what happens.

SIMPLE ABUNDANCE
OCTOBER 29

receives negative impulses, it duplicates in your daily round whatever it is instructed to manifest.

What are the alternatives to worry? First, calculate whether you have enough money for all your needs *today.* If you do, stop focusing on lack this minute.

Anytime you have more than you need, you have abundance. Catch yourself the next time you start dwelling on what you don't have; switch tracks by noticing and appreciating all you do have. As this becomes a personal habit, you'll find yourself coping well with any amount of money you have, rather than worrying about it.

Worry is a future-tense emotion. Worry is a projection of a possible—not necessarily probable—scenario. *Will* there be enough? Where *will* it come from? How long *will* it last?

Sanaya Roman and Duane Packer, in *Creating Money: Keys to Abundance,* suggest that instead of worrying, you should "Ask yourself, 'How can I *create* money today?'" What actions can you take to create money?

Our authenticity is found hidden in the small details of our daily round—home, family, work, pleasures.

SOMETHING MORE
"SMALL THINGS
FORGOTTEN"

"There is an enormous difference in the energy you send out to the universe when you focus on creating money rather than needing money; the first is magnetic to money and the latter is not," Roman and Packer explain. "Constant worry about money blocks your creativity and clear thinking."

We should remember that all financial transactions really boil down to an exchange of energy. Someone provides us with energy in the form of work and we reciprocate by paying for those services through energy in the form of money, which we've earned by the sweat of our own brow.

Joe Dominguez and Vicki Robin, authors of *Your Money or Your Life,* a guide to achieving financial independence by transforming your relationship to money, tell us, "Money is something we choose to trade our life energy for. Our life energy is our allotment of time here on earth, the hours of precious life available to us . . . it is limited and irretrievable . . . our choices about how we use it express the meaning and purpose of our time here on earth." Keeping track of how you spend your life energy or your money is a very illuminating exercise; try keeping a record, not of money, but of the time that worrying about money intrudes upon your life. This may help you to better evaluate decisions about when to spend.

Authentic success is internal. Often, other people aren't even aware at first that you've reached it. The moment of success is the awareness that "I can do it" or "I have done it." And it's comforting to know that this can't be taken away from you by an external event.

SOMETHING MORE
"AUTHENTIC
SUCCESS"

Becoming More Magnetic to Money

I have come to believe that giving and receiving are really the same. Giving and receiving—not giving and taking.

JOYCE GRENFELL

Spiritual law, no matter which path, tells us that as we give, so shall we receive. We realize that money is a form of energy, and energy does not increase if it's hoarded. Energy must circulate freely for power to be released. When we receive an increase of money in our lives, giving away a portion of that money keeps the channels of abundance circulating freely, as Spirit intended.

Giving is what keeps the abundance cycle in constant motion in our lives. The mechanism by which I have transformed my life is through tithing. Tithing is returning to God "a tenth" of all the money you receive and regularly donating it to a spiritual or a nonprofit organization that carries on Spirit's work in the world by caring for those unable to care for themselves—the sick, the hungry, the homeless.

Before *Simple Abundance* was published I had very little money and was constantly focused on lack. As I've said before, skeptics make the best seekers, so in my attempt to change my relationship to money I became will-

221

ing to conduct a little fiscal experiment. I began tithing out of my grocery money.

Very soon after I began tithing, I noticed some interesting test results. Even though I was giving money away, the disposable cash that remained seemed to last longer. It stretched; I was able to consistently save for the first time. I also started to relax because I felt that a spiritual contract had been made and I was holding up my end of an ancient biblical bargain.

In the Old Testament Book of Malachi (31:11) God invites us to take a spiritual silent partner who has a personal interest in our prosperity. We are told, "Bring ye all the tithes into the storehouse, that there may be meat and wine in My house, and prove me herewith . . . if I will not open up the windows of heaven, and pour out so many blessings upon you, that there shall not be room enough to receive it." Since I was making good on my promise, I felt confident that Heaven would honor its end, which always happened.

Still, there would be times when I would panic and think, "I don't have enough to give away," and I wouldn't. Sure enough, some "unexpected" expense would occur that same week that was usually more costly than my tithe would have been—the car would break down, the cat would need an emergency visit to the vet, my daughter's growth spurt rendered her new winter coat useless overnight. Coincidence? Maybe. But I don't think so.

Since tithing has become so fundamental to how I conduct my life and my work, I'm frequently asked

We all desperately want to believe that money makes all the difference. But when your heart is broken, it doesn't matter whether the pillow you sob into is cotton or silk damask.

SOMETHING MORE
"KEEPING BODY AND
SOUL TOGETHER"

about it by people who are having money challenges. I reassure them that there really is a cycle of giving and receiving and that they, like me, will benefit from it, while experiencing the great feeling that comes from sharing the good that comes our way.

There is no scarcity except in our souls.

Chapter 11 — Moodlings

Authentic Success

1. What connections in your life induce passion and make you feel truly awake and alive? Note here the first things that occur to you. How can you incorporate these things into your work?

2. Our priorities should be flexible and they should change as we do. We need to identify what is truly important in our lives. What are your priorities right now?

3. Look at your list. Which priorities reflect what you feel you should be doing and which reflect your honest passions? Are you even on your own list? If not, what are you doing this week to put yourself there?

4. Describe your definition of authentic success in three sentences.

5. What does money truly mean to you? How much of this has to do with the way your parents viewed money? Think about their patterns of spending and saving and contrast them with your own.

6. Now that you have determined your attitude toward money, think about how you would like your children or loved ones to feel about it. How can you instill these values in them?

7.   Tithing is a powerful but somewhat daunting concept. It sometimes helps to focus on the good you would like to be able to do before you actually commit to it. List five charities that you feel passionate about, and think of one thing your money could do to help each one:

Now when it comes time to set aside money each month, you will have a better idea of where it is going, and this will help fuel your resolve.

8.   Are you willing to give tithing a fair chance? Try an experiment and tithe for the next month. What do you have to lose besides misery and lack? Keep a record of your experiment here.

Write Your Way into Wholeness

Never Wish More Than You Work

It will never rain roses: When we want to have
more roses we must plant more trees.

George Eliot

Chapter 12

Becoming Real

*Always be a first-rate version of yourself,
instead of a second-rate version of somebody else.*

JUDY GARLAND

Many people are aware of Margery Williams's wonderful children's classic *The Velveteen Rabbit,* about how a little boy's love made his toy velveteen bunny grow into a real rabbit. But not many people know that the book itself became enduringly "real" in a similar way.

The book was published in 1928, and afterward it faded nearly into oblivion. Decades later a minister preached a sermon about the lessons of *The Velveteen Rabbit* in his church. Soon the publisher's phone began to ring with demands for copies, so the book went back to press after all those years, and word spread that it was wonderful. People read it and loved it and made it real again.

Do you know the story of the Velveteen Rabbit? One Christmas morning he was found sitting in the top of a little boy's stocking with a sprig of holly between his paws. The little boy was enchanted and played with the rabbit for two whole hours until the family directed his attention to all the other wonderful playthings he'd gotten as gifts, and the Velveteen Rabbit was forgotten.

For a long time the bunny remained just another toy in the nursery. But he didn't mind because he was able to carry on long philosophical discussions with the old Skin Horse, who was very wise and experienced in the strange ways of nursery magic. One of the rabbit's favorite topics of conversation was on becoming "Real" like the animals in the nearby forest.

The Skin Horse patiently explained to the bunny that "Real isn't how you are made. It's a thing that happens to you. When a child loves you for a long, long time, not just to play with, but *really* loves you, then you become real."

But becoming Real doesn't happen overnight in the nursery or on the path to authenticity. "Generally by the time you are Real, most of your hair has been loved off, and your eyes drop out and you get all loose in the joints and very shabby. But these things don't matter at all, because once you are Real, you can't be ugly except to people who don't understand."

Like the Velveteen Rabbit, we long to become Real, to know what authenticity feels like.

One of the ways we do this is by growing gradually into our true selves. As you learn to acknowledge, accept, and appreciate what it is that makes you different from all the other women in the world, the process begins. As you learn to trust the wisdom of your heart and summon up the courage to make creative choices based on what you know is right for you, process becomes progress. As you learn to endow even the smallest moment of each day with Love, even those in which you make mistakes, progress becomes reality perfected. Real Life.

Transforming progress into reality perfected is what my friend the modern dance teacher does, with her sharp eyes—she looks through a student's skin and muscles, to the very center of the person.

"Work from your center," she tells the group. "A tree sloughs off its bark, but sap comes from the center. Your life force is at your center. Hold yourself from your center. Hold in your abdomen, push up with your rotator muscles, not from your feet. Hold from your center, from the life force."

In order to be true to our creative selves, we must journey to our center. Past the conscious sentries in the brain, beyond the barbed wire barricades of the heart, into the trenches of "truth or dare." Your mind might be able to pretend you're someone you're not, but your body can't. There is a Shaker axiom that says, "Be what you seem to be, and seem to be what you really are." This is what it means to live authentically.

What matters, what is Real, is the contentment of our souls. Because it is through the small details of everyday life that we make our souls feel welcome.

Today, ask your Soul what she requires to make her earthly stay with you more pleasurable. Ask, "What do you need at this moment? What would bring you peace, contentment, joy?" It may be to slow down, take a walk, hug a child, caress a cat. Flip through a magazine. What-

The more we allow ourselves to recognize the wisdom and truth in spiritual paths, the closer to Wholeness we become.

SIMPLE ABUNDANCE
DECEMBER 6

ever it might be, she will tell you. Ask. Right now. What does she say?

Half-Answered Prayers

God answers sharp and sudden on some prayers,
And thrusts the thing we have prayed for in our face,
A gauntlet with a gift in it.

ELIZABETH BARRETT BROWNING

Whether we realize it or not, with every breath, with every heartbeat, women pray. Everyday life is the prayer—how we conduct it, celebrate it, consecrate it.

In its purest form, prayer is conversation. Communion. Connection. Intimacy. Prayer is the dialect of Divinity.

Oscar Wilde believed that there were only two tragedies in life: not getting what you pray for and getting it.

"Answered prayers are scary," Julia Cameron admits in her marvelous book *The Artist's Way*, which honors creativity as a spiritual path. "They imply responsibility. You asked for it. Now that you've got it, what are you going to do? Why else the cautionary phrase, 'Watch out for what you pray for; you just might get it'? Answered prayers deliver us back to our own hand. This is not comfortable."

Very often the reason we're uncomfortable is because we've not been praying for the right thing, and on some deep level we know it. We pray for a promotion at work when what we really should pray for is the courage to seek our calling; we pray for worldly success when what we really long for is an awareness of the riches that surround us daily. We pray for a specific outcome in any given situation, when what our souls cry for is serenity, no matter what happens.

When we get a no in answer to our prayers we are rarely envisioning the big picture; nor are we weighing our requests against the more dire needs of others that are not apparent to us.

Actually, our prayers are always being answered. We just don't like to think that "no" is a reasonable response to our very reasonable requests. If we didn't need it would we be asking for it? Writer Madeleine L'Engle confesses in her memoir *The Irrational Season*—surely speaking for us all—"We don't like the Noes; and sometimes we like the Noes of God less than any other No."

Once during a season of personal bewilderment I prayed every conceivable way I knew how for help, guidance, and direction concerning a close relationship. It's highs and lows were driving me wild with grief. My enormous mood swings, which depended on whether my lover was giving or withholding affection, affected every other aspect of my life, including my health and work. Most days I'd pray that we would live happily ever after, but often I would pray that Spirit would help me fall out of love with him. Eventually it got to the point where I didn't care what the outcome was, I just wanted peace of mind. Finally the relationship ended. Badly. I was left with a broken heart, a shattered soul, and engulfed by a deep estrangement from God, who I felt had turned a silent ear to my prayers. It was the spiritual crucible of my life. I never felt more lost or lonely.

My enforced spiritual estrangement lasted about a week because my relationship to Spirit is the most passionate and important one I have. However, I was still wounded and angry and wasn't thankful for much of anything. So in a fit of pique I started a new Gratitude Journal, "Being Thankful for the Noes of God." I was, of course, being facetious, but I thought I'd write down every day one reason I was grateful that God had dashed one of my dreams by saying no to a particular prayer. Although I didn't feel grateful at these moments, I knew it was crucial to express it and bless the situation I secretly cursed before I could move on.

Now, I wish that I could tell you that within a week my lover learned the error of his ways and returned, begging for forgiveness. No such luck. But what did happen was that by focusing each day on a hidden gift from that tortuous relationship, and thanking Heaven for not answering my desperate supplications, I learned what Stella Terrill Mann meant when she said, "No sincere prayer leaves us where it finds us."

It doesn't matter how awareness arrives. What matters is that it comes.

SIMPLE ABUNDANCE
JANUARY 13

234

When your prayers seem delayed or denied, you need to ask Spirit if you're praying for the right thing. If you're not, ask that the right prayer might be revealed to you. Often when we hear a no, it's really a "not yet" to allow us more time, space, wisdom, and experience to prepare for the glorious moment when we're finally ready to hear Spirit say, "Yes!"

Your Spiritual Journey

Spirituality is basically our relationship with reality.

CHANDRA PATEL

Throughout my life I have loved exploring other spiritual traditions in addition to my own. At first I was a little nervous, going to other places of worship. But then I recast my curiosity as an adventure. "An adventure is a transgression you don't regret," the travel writer Kate Wheeler explains. "True adventure starts with desire, an inclination to enter the unknown. In hopes of finding what? More of yourself, or of the world? Yes. . . . During an adventure you experience a peculiar mental state, thrilled, and open to surprise."

But I invited my surprises gently. First I went to a Quaker meeting; then to a synagogue. Then I went to many different Protestant denominations to try to distinguish the difference, for example, between the Southern Baptists and Presbyterians.

And then I ventured where I had always wanted to go—to a Pentecostal church with an entirely black congregation. I love gospel music, and for a while I attended that church, reveling in the rich, wonderful music. People would get up and testify (which is to publicly describe something Spirit made happen in their lives), and everyone else would respond "Amen." I was the only white person there, but I was embraced absolutely. I loved the Sunday services so much that I even started going to Wednesday night services too, so I could hear those Amens.

One day I too got up to testify to God's miraculous working in my own life, and I heard Amen, Amen, Amen. This public testimony freed me, and I've been testifying about the joys of spiritual life in many ways ever since.

"In undertaking a spiritual life, what matters is simple," American Buddhist master and teacher Jack Kornfield tells us in his wonderful book *A Path with Heart: A Guide through the Perils and Promises of Spiritual Life.* "We must make certain that our path is connected with our heart. . . . We discover that no one can define for us exactly what our path should be. Instead, we must allow the mystery and beauty of this question to resonate with our being. Then somewhere within us an answer will come and understanding will arise. If we are still and listen deeply, even for a moment, we will know if we are following a path with heart."

When you are exploring other spiritual traditions you can let the images and the language draw you in. Even if they are alien to you, they may speak to you on a

Sometimes we choose tracks left by others that plant us right back where we started from; sometimes they are our own tracks. But invariably, if we keep on going, picking ourselves up each time we stumble, we learn the joy of delayed gratification. We look back and see, like an oasis, the Wilderness as a fertile place after all.

SOMETHING MORE
"CROSSING THE
THRESHOLD"

soul level. When I am praying in a synagogue, I don't have to understand Hebrew to be moved by the beauty of the prayers. As the dancer Gelsey Kirkland admits, "In saying my prayers, I discovered the voice of an inner-most self, the raw nerve of my identity."

Many of us have believed all our lives that choosing a spiritual path was all about submission, sacrifice, and suffering, and that only the worldly path could provide freedom and good fortune. If this is still your fear, ask yourself this:

Have any of the world's gifts given you authentic happiness? Has even the most perfect job, relationship, house, money fulfilled you for long?

How many times have we waited for Spirit to move for us, when in fact Spirit is waiting to work *with* us?

Getting Real

You can do more than praying after you've prayed. You can never do more than praying before you have prayed.

CORRIE TEN BLOOM

The mystic knows that an untold number of variables interact to influence how our days will flow in the dance we call life. The way things happen, opportunities that present themselves, how we react, our very thoughts are inextricably interwoven with our relationships, families, friends, associates, and the unknown forces that surround us," Rabbi David A. Cooper writes in his beautiful book *God Is a Verb*. "For, more than we realize, our lives hinge on little things: one telephone call, a letter, a thoughtful gesture, even a nod or a smile at just the right moment."

One hinge that holds together a woman's sanity is solitude, but it isn't a little hinge. It's huge.

It took me a long time to realize that solitude had to be woven into the fabric of my daily life. After I had been taking creative excursions for a few weeks, I began to feel more content. I wasn't as moody. I had more patience, tolerance and felt more outgoing. Solitude—deliberately pulling away from others to go toward my self—seemed to increase my ability to bestow the thoughtful gestures that mean so much—the telephone call, letter, conversation, smile at just the right moment.

I began to wonder—if this was the emotional return on the investment of just two hours a week, what would my life be like if I invested an hour a day in my own tranquillity? It was a wild and crazy thought. Subversive, really.

Which is exactly how I started to introduce more "self time" into my schedule. By bookending my day with a half hour in the morning and a half hour in the evening, no one but my soul noticed. In the morning I'd just sit in silence and have my first cup of tea before anyone else in the house was up; in the evening I'd withdraw as early as I could manage comfortably and reflect on the day that had just passed. Had I lived it? Before solitude became my most congenial companion that hadn't even been a question. I know how busy you are, but I guarantee that you can siphon moments of solitude every day. Early morning, late night. Coffee break, lunch hour. Your little one's naptime. Commuting. Walking. Waiting in line. Instead of watching television. Instead of making one more commitment. Instead of doing chores (don't worry, they'll wait for you).

In the beginning I didn't know what silence sounded like. Now I know there are many kinds—that silence is a symphony. There are pregnant pauses, anticipatory silences, introductory silences, silent resolutions, silent agreements. Silent clarity.

Does your alarm clock sound like a starting gun? Do you race through your days, wishing for more hours to do more things without even realizing that what you really long for are more hours to do less? Do you crawl back into bed at night exhausted and empty? Does the dawn find you drained by the daily tug between personal wants versus family needs, or domestic responsibilities versus work obligations? Why is it that no matter how you've tried, you just haven't been able to shorten the to-do list? So stop trying. Instead of struggling to control the outside influences on your life, start on the inside.

How? The key is mindfulness, the ancient practice that teaches us how to live in the present moment, which is perhaps the most powerful way to slow down the relentless pace of our lives. Being mindful also reduces stress, increases creativity, encourages intuition, deep-

See if you can't give yourself the gift of one hour a day to journey within. You need enough breathing space to allow your heart to ponder what is precious. Or perhaps you can let your imagination soar to the twilight where dreams first dwell.

SIMPLE ABUNDANCE
JANUARY 26

239

ens your connection to yourself, and strengthens your sense of spirituality, which is truly your relationship to reality.

So why aren't you doing it? Probably because for many women it seems foreign and intimidating. The Buddhists have likened the untrained mind to a monkey that swings wildly from branch to branch, never settling in one spot. It's an apt comparison for most of us, but we don't even realize how unfocused our thoughts are because we keep our bodies moving at such a furious pace. We dash so quickly from one task to the next, striving to fulfill desires, meet deadlines, achieve goals, or keep pace that we are hardly even aware of the task we're doing. Unlearning those old habits requires practice, patience, perseverance, but most of all awareness.

Mindfulness means that instead of thinking about what you've just done, should have done, or are about to do, you focus only on what you're doing right now, whether it's reading a book, driving to work, paying bills, cooking dinner, picking up the dry cleaning, or bathing your child. Mindfulness means not being so impatient that you try to open a stubborn orange juice container with a steak knife. Because unless you pay attention to that fleeting moment, you'll lose a pint of blood on the kitchen floor and five hours in the emergency room.

In Thornton Wilder's play *Our Town* a deeply poignant scene takes place in a graveyard. Ghosts comfort the young heroine, who has recently died in childbirth. Emily grieves over the life she has just left and asks to revisit just one ordinary unimportant day in her life. When she gets her wish, she realizes how much the living take for granted.

"I didn't realize," she confesses mournfully, "all that was going on and we never noticed . . . clocks ticking . . . and Mama's sunflowers. And food and coffee. And new-ironed dresses and hot baths . . . and sleeping and waking up. Oh, earth, you're too wonderful for anybody to realize you."

What about your life is so wonderful that you have scarcely been able to realize it? I hope, after the time we've spent together, that *you,* in all your glorious imperfections, top this list.

Life is made up of millions of moments. You must experience each one before you can appreciate them. Whether you're shampooing your hair, having an argument, writing a memo, making love, talking on the telephone, or eating an apple, savor the sensations involved. All of these moments, whether joyous, routine, or painful, deserve your full attention. In a life well lived, they are the heartbeats.

Chapter 12 — Moodlings

Becoming Real

1. How many peaceful interludes do you take for yourself each day? What are they?

2. Had nothing to write down for the exercise above? Do take this personally! What is one new break you can carve out for yourself?

3. On the Simple Abundance path we seek everyday epiphanies—occasions when we can experience the sacred in the ordinary. Describe a time when you became aware that no day is unimportant:

4.   Being authentic or becoming Real means pushing past your comfort zone in your thinking and in your behavior. When was the last time you did this? When you remember it, what feeling comes back to you? Fear? Astonishment? In what way has pushing past your comfort zone become easier each time you do it?

5.   In the first chapter of this book, you wrote down ten words that defined you. Without looking back at that list, note now whatever comes to mind—ten words that describe you:

6.   When was the last time you prayed for something and felt that your prayer went unanswered? Looking back now, did you actually just get an answer you weren't looking for? What was it?

7. When did you thank Spirit for answering one of your prayers with a "no," or "not yet"? How is your life better because Heaven knows more than you did?

8. What other spiritual tradition intrigues you? What's stopping you from exploring it? Could you push past your comfort zone to give it a try? If not, why?

9. Each day how do you serve Spirit in some task you perform? What is it? (Hint: It does not take place in your normal house of worship, but in your home, out in nature, at work, and in your daily round.)

10. How are you being truthful to your own creativity? Can you see yourself as a mystic of the everyday? In what way?

Write Your Way into Wholeness

Can You Feel a Pulse?

It's exhilarating to be alive in a time of awakening consciousness;
it can also be confusing, disorienting, and painful.

Adrienne Rich

245

Afterword

The last part of any Simple Abundance workshop is our wrap-up session, where we review the lessons, share last thoughts, exchange addresses, and make promises to keep in touch.

Virginia Woolf once said that the challenge of any lecturer was not to change the world but merely to provide each audience member one provocative thought to write down, put upon their mantel and mull over. One life-changing thought is quite enough for any of us to take in on any given day. If you've found even just one new thing to ponder from our time together on these pages, then you're off to a good start to transforming authenticity from a concept to your own spiritual path.

Here's a thought from each of these chapters for your mantel mulling.

Chapter One
The most important promise you'll ever keep is to love yourself into Wholeness.

Chapter Two
Gratitude is essential to living the good life.

Chapter Three
The time, creative energy, and emotion you invest in self-nurturance will produce priceless personal dividends.

Afterword

Chapter Four

You are a phenomenal woman.

Say it aloud every day.

I am a phenomenal woman.

Say it until you believe it.

Chapter Five

The more risks you take, the luckier you become.

Chapter Six

Simplicity does not mean making do with less,
but appreciating the important things more.

Chapter Seven

Big change comes with small choices.

Chapter Eight

To play is to let the Universe know you're willing
to learn your life lessons through joy.

Chapter Nine

Nothing hurts you more than your expectations
of how "it" should be.

Chapter Ten

Our relationships are only as emotionally healthy,
happy, holy, and content as we are.

Chapter Eleven

Authentic success is living without regret.

Chapter Twelve

Authenticity is the most personal form of worship.

Cinematherapy

As far as I'm concerned, movies fall into only two categories: spiritual mentors or self-medication. "Studying movies for their mystical messages empowers us. We gain insight and great self-awareness," Marsha Sinetar suggests in her fascinating book *Reel Power: Spiritual Growth through Film*. "So much of life today is centered on problems, recovery, and the painful struggles of trying to meet the unrelenting demands of twenty-first century living. Unfortunately, by dwelling only on problems, and thus failing to see ourselves in a heroic, promising light, we limit ourselves. Movies elevate our sights, enlarge our imagination. Film, like poetry, is one of our heart's most subtle agents. It reminds us of what we know, helps us stretch and change, provides us with a sensory catalyst for creative cutting-edge change."

Change of mood often requires another kind of sensory catalyst, hunkering down in the dark with a box or a bowl of popcorn—a surefire home remedy for whatever ails you. "As we women know, movies are more than entertainment: They're self-medication," Nancy Peske and Beverly West write in their witty and wise reference tome *Cinematherapy: The Girl's Guide to Movies for Every Mood*. "A good flick is like a soothing tonic that, if administered properly, in combination with total inertia and something obscenely high in fat grams, can cure everything from an identity crisis to a bad hair day to the I-hate-my-job blues."

Creating a reel-life rescue vault by starting a personal movie archive that caters to your every mood is very restorative and rewarding. Over the next year, create your own resource list. Stock up with chick flicks that affirm the loyalty of gal pals, tearjerkers to induce therapeutic crying jags, goofy comedies to make you laugh till your sides hurt, and epics that inspire and uplift. Here are suggestions of movies I've mined for golden insights. Many of these are classics that have been recently re-released on video and are worth tracking down.

Chapter 1: Welcome to You

A Room with a View (1986) Playing a young woman seeking marriage and a stable home, Helena Bonham Carter must decide between the sensible, composed man who can provide security and an impulsive, passionate man.

Senso (1954) Upper-class Venetian woman Alida Valli seeks revenge after being betrayed by an officer in the army for whom she had risked everything.

Two for the Road (1967) Driving around in France while volleying smart remarks and harsh criticisms, married couple Audrey Hepburn and Albert Finney portray a marriage surviving because of an accustomed reliance on each other.

Chapter 2: The Fullness of Life

Holiday (1938) Cary Grant, a young, unusual millionaire, is brought home to the family of his fiancée, where it becomes apparent that his true love will be the sister, Katharine Hepburn.

Moonstruck (1987) Opposites attract in this relationship between Cher and Nicolas Cage, who are dissimilar in every way except for their shared love.

Life Is Beautiful (1997) Roberto Benigni directs and stars alongside Nicoletta Braschi in this emotional story of a passionate romance and a devoted family during the Holocaust.

Chapter 3: Romancing the Soul

A Man and a Woman (1966) The amazing love story of a young widow (Anouk Aimée) and a young widower (Jean-Louis Tritignant) unfolds in this romantic drama.

Love in the Afternoon (1957) Audrey Hepburn falls in love with the older, wealthier Gary Cooper in this clever romance directed and cowritten by Billy Wilder.

Summertime (1955) At long last, while vacationing in Venice, Katharine Hepburn finds Mr. Right (Rossano Brazzi). Unfortunately, he's already married.

Chapter 4: Phenomenal Woman

Jane Eyre (1944) Based on the novel about an orphaned girl who matures into a strong young woman (Joan Fontaine) and lives a great love story when she falls in love with Mr. Rochester (Orson Welles).

Mrs. Soffel (1984) Based on a true story. Diane Keaton plays a prison warden's wife, Mrs. Soffel, counseling a convicted murderer, Mel Gibson, only to assist him in escaping after they fall in love.

The English Patient (1996) Ralph Fiennes and Kristin Scott-Thomas act in this World War II romantic drama about a young nurse caring for a gruesomely burned patient whose story of a passionate, adulterous affair is revealed through flashbacks.

Chapter 5: Courage

Witness (1985) Despite their conflicting worlds, Harrison Ford and Kelly McGillis are brought together and begin a romance that transcends their differences and transforms each of them.

One Way Passage (1932) As Kay Francis and William Powell begin a romance they keep their secrets to themselves: one is suffering from a terminal disease and the other is a criminal going to prison.

Casablanca (1942) Rick (Humphrey Bogart) and Ilsa (Ingrid Bergman) try to find a way for their love to survive their conflicting beliefs during World War II.

Chapter 6: The House of Belonging

The Enchanted Cottage (1945) In the enchanted cottage a deformed man (Robert Young) and a plain woman (Dorothy McGuire) are able to find the true beauty in each other.

The Ghost and Mrs. Muir (1947) In a cottage in England, a lonely widow (Gene Tierney) is romantically haunted by the ghost of a sea captain (Rex Harrison).

Make Way for Tomorrow (1937) An elderly couple married for fifty years want only to live together for the rest of their lives but are instead separated by their children and forced to live in different houses.

Chapter 7: Choice As a Spiritual Gift

It Happened One Night (1934) Claudette Colbert rebels against her father by romancing a young boy, only to discover later that she is destined to fall in love with hardworking Clark Gable.

Sense and Sensibility (1995) Emma Thompson and Kate Winslet star in this adaptation of Jane Austen's novel about two sisters and their widowed mother who are left in poverty after their father dies.

When Harry Met Sally (1989) Harry (Billy Crystal) and Sally (Meg Ryan) must decide how to preserve their treasured friendship and not allow sex to come between them.

Chapter 8: The Love of Play

Zorba the Greek (1964) An Englishman (Alan Bates) living an existence devoid of excitement is transformed after discovering he has an inheritance on a small Greek island where he also meets Zorba (Anthony Quinn), a Greek living a life full of pleasure.

Roman Holiday (1953) Despite their conflicting worlds, Gregory Peck and Audrey Hepburn are brought together, begin a romance, and make a surprising decision about their love and their lives.

Breakfast at Tiffany's (1961) Audrey Hepburn and George Peppard play two characters who allude themselves in different ways and discover they are not yet truly who they want to be.

Chapter 9: Learning to Let Go

Immortal Beloved (1994) After the great composer's death, Ludwig van Beethoven's mentor struggles to discern the identity of Beethoven's "Immortal Beloved" while dealing with his will and testament.

Waterloo Bridge (1940) Vivien Leigh is forced from her life as a ballerina when the family of her lover ostracizes her after the lover is killed in an accident, only to discover later that he is not dead.

Letter from an Unknown Woman (1948) Joan Fontaine portrays a young girl who develops a disastrous, lifelong crush on an attractive pianist, Louis Jordan.

Chapter 10: Sacred Connections

Sleepless in Seattle (1993) Sam (Tom Hanks) decides not to look for another companion after his wife dies. However, his eight-year-old son decides differently, and through a national radio show finds the perfect woman, Annie (Meg Ryan), for his father.

Somewhere in Time (1980) An emotional story of a miserable playwright (Christopher Reeve) who is able to travel backward in time to find the actress (Jane Seymour) whose portrait he fell in love with.

Out of Africa (1985) Set in Africa. Meryl Streep plays Isak Dinesen and Robert Redford her soul mate Denys Finch-Hatton as they experience a passionate affair.

Chapter 11: Authentic Success

Sounder (1972) Cicely Tyson and Paul Winfield find their healthy marriage and happy family challenged by the trying times of the Great Depression.

The Shop Around the Corner (1940) James Stewart and Margaret Sullivan are simultaneously arguing coworkers and loving pen pals (though they don't know it) who finally realize they're made for each other.

A Star Is Born (1954) Judy Garland, an actress on the brink of stardom, and James Mason, a declining actor, act out the romantic drama of the stereotypical tragic Hollywood marriage.

Chapter 12: Becoming Real

Brief Encounter (1945) In this dramatic movie a passionate but brief romance begins after two strangers, Celia Johnson and Trevor Howard, who are already married to others, meet at a train station.

Love Affair (1939) Irene Dunne and Charles Boyer meet and fall in love despite their engagements to other people and must separate to discover if their love is true or not.

Emma (1996) Perhaps because she is always playing matchmaker for others, Emma (Gwyneth Paltrow) is not even aware of her own romantic feelings toward a certain Mr. Knightley until she attempts to unite him with a friend.

Audiotherapy

S ince the dawn of humanity, spiritual healers known as shamans have used sound to drive disease from the body, depression from the mind, despair from the soul. Because music reaches beyond the barriers of our conscious mind, it is a powerful ally for inner work. Gradually building a personal collection of different music selections helps you collect your thoughts, calms you down, channels your creative energy, and calls forth your authentic gifts.

But very often we get in a rut, even with our pleasures. Sure, piano nocturnes soothe you, but so can jazz. Not, however, if you've never listened to it because "it's not you." It has been my experience that accessing my authenticity is more fun when I'll admit I haven't a clue as to what might move me and I'm open to the new. Listening to unfamiliar music is one of my favorite methods of jump-starting a new ecstatic experience. Here's a sampler of sound tastes that have become my personal soul soothers—I've divided them by category, because only you know what fits the mood you're in, but try to create categories for yourself to match a whole range of moods.

Swing and Standards

Frank Sinatra—*Songs for Swinging Lovers*

Benny Goodman Live at Carnegie Hall

The Complete Ella Fitzgerald and Louis Armstrong

Bossa Nova and Latin

Songs from the Heart of Cuba

Carlos Jobim, Stan Getz, and João Gilberto

100% Azucar: The Best of Celia Cruz

Bossa Brava—Volumes II, III

Country

Patsy Cline's Greatest Hits

Wynonna Collection

The Women of Country (Lifetime Music Compilation)

Opera

Andrea Bocelli—*Aria: The Opera Album*

Prima Diva (compilation including Maria Callas, Elisabeth Schwarzkopf, Kiri Te Kanawa, Jessye Norman)

3 Tenors: Carreras, Domingo, Pavarotti in Concert

DivaSoprana at the Movies: Lesley Garrett

Cecilia Bartoli—*Live in Italy*

Blues

The Voice of the Sparrow: Very Best of Edith Piaf

The Women of Soul (Lifetime Music Compilation)

Billie Holiday—*Lady Sings the Blues*

Etta James—*Heart of a Woman*

Jazz

The Jazz Masters

Sarah Vaughan

The Essential Nina Simone

Film Soundtracks and Showtunes

The English Patient

Out of Africa

A Walk on the Moon

The Premiere Collection: The Best of Andrew Lloyd Webber

Mel Tormé at the Movies

Secret Garden

Classical

Pachelbel Canon and Other Baroque Favorites

Kelly Yost: Piano Reflections

Michael Hoppe / Tim Wheater: The Yearning Romances for Alto Flute

Rock and Roll

Sting—*Mercury Falling, Brand New Day*

Tina Turner—*Simply the Best*

Women of Rock (Lifetime Music Compilation)

Girl Friends

Randy Crawford—*Every Kind of Mood*

A Century of Women's Music (Lifetime Music Compilation)

Black Pearls—The Poetry of Maya Angelou

Sarah Brightman—*Eden*

Mary Chapin Carpenter—*Party Doll*

World Music

Voce: Music from Women of the World

Loreena McKennit—*Parallel Dreams*

Best of the Clannad

Madredeus—*O Espirito Da Paz*

Folk Music

Joan Baez—*Diamonds and Rust*

Nanci Griffith—*Other Voices, Other Rooms*

Cheryl Wheeler—*The Sylvia Hotel*

Lounge

Manhattan Transfer

Mabel Mercer Sings Cole Porter

Cocktail Mix (Vols. 1–4, Rhino music compilation)

Bibliotherapy

When I was going down emotionally for the third time, other people's words have been the life preservers that kept me afloat. Beloved books are as individual as fingerprints. These titles come from my own bookshelf and are suggested to either pique your interest or prime your creative well. That's why keeping your own resource is so valuable. A great resource is *500 Great Books by Women: A Reader's Guide* (Penguin). Look for it in any large library.

A way to make bibliotherapy part of your daily round is to keep a pleasure reading list, with poetry, memoirs, meaty fiction, whatever you've been curious about or dying to dip into but haven't had the time to sample. Coax yourself into leaving all that brain-numbing, eye-glazing work-related material behind and pull out one of your pleasure reads while waiting in line at the bank, lolling in the bath, or commuting. Time that was once seen as wasted will be transformed into wonderful moments of opportunity and transcendence.

John O'Donohue

Readers frequently ask whose books I read as sources of solace and inspiration. The works of my dear friend John O'Donohue, the Irish poet, scholar, and philosopher, are never far from my desk or bedside. In his words, I hear the voice of the Divine.

> *Anam Cara: A Book of Celtic Wisdom* (HarperCollins) Exquisitely written reflections blending philosophy, poetry, and spirituality that explore

the mystery of our anam caras, those "soul friends" who love us into full beings and lead us to our Divine destiny—learning how to Love ourselves unconditionally.

Eternal Echoes: Exploring Our Yearning to Belong (HarperCollins/Cliff Street) Addresses our soul's deepest calling, to "belong," and why this Divine restlessness must be honored before we can experience true happiness.

I am a deeply devout, hopeful romantic and the following two books are my favorite novels. Read them in this order and then make note of your feelings and emotional responses.

Graham Greene

The End of the Affair (Penguin Twentieth-Century Classics) (Penguin USA) A haunting novel of obsession versus redemption written in the fifties that wonders whether or not we must choose between faith and passion.

Niall Williams

Four Letters of Love (Warner) A contemporary Irish novel that explores the same theme but concludes "the plots of God and Love are the same."

Diane Ackerman

Want a college education in the comfort of your own home? Read Diane Ackerman's books. Poet, scholar, scientist, explorer, renaissance woman. Diane's the woman I want to be when I grow up.

A Natural History of the Senses (Vintage) Delves into the mystery of the five senses, offering a new appreciation for the gifts of smell, touch, vision, hearing, and taste.

A Natural History of Love (Vintage) Beginning with the ancient worlds of the Egyptians, Greeks, and Romans, the history of love is told through a scientific, philosophical, and psychological perspective and engaging narrative.

Deep Play (Random House) Describes how playing is a vital part of life's grand plan, not meant to be abandoned as we age but embraced so that we might evolve into spiritual as well as human beings.

Elizabeth Bowen

Bowen, the elegant Anglo-Irish writer, was popular from the thirties through the fifties and seems to be the literary link between Virginia Woolf and contemporary English writers such as Iris Murdock and Anita Brookner. Her beautiful novels and short stories center on women torn between tradition and their own self-fulfillment and are usually set against the background of war.

Collected Stories (Ecco)

The Last September (Penguin Twentieth-Century Classics) (Viking)

The House in Paris (Penguin Twentieth-Century Classics) (Penguin USA)

To the North (Penguin Twentieth-Century Classics) (Penguin USA)

Bowen's Court The history of the author's family and the story of her childhood in Dublin, Ireland.

Merle Shain

A Canadian writer, Merle Shain left us all too soon. I grieve again over our literary loss every time I reread her, which is annually. Her wise and gentle reflections on the mysteries of love, written in the seventies, are frequently the antidote for whatever relationship woe ails me. Sadly, her books are all out of print now, but well worth the search in used bookstores.

Some Men Are More Perfect Than Others

When Lovers Are Friends

Courage My Love

Hearts That We Broke Long Ago

Laurie Colwin

She was a writer's writer, a kitchen mystic, and my best page pal until she left us. The day I learned Laurie died I spent the morning making and eating her recipe for gingerbread, in between blowing my nose, rereading her books, praying, and mourning her loss. Still do, but at least I have her books, which are now published by Harper Perennial Library.

Home Cooking: A Writer in the Kitchen

More Home Cooking: A Writer Returns to the Kitchen

Family Happiness: A Novel

Goodbye without Leaving

Happy All the Time: A Novel

Passion and Affect

Another Marvelous Thing

Barrie Dolnick

Barrie Dolnick is one of the most generous people I know. She not only believes everyone is entitled to their hearts' desires, she's willing to help us get it. Her enchanting books—which update ancient practices for attracting emotional fulfillment, prosperity, success, and harmony at home—are personal favorites. Barrie helps us find the mystical in the mundane. Her wisdom and delightful advice are blessings.

Simple Spells for Love (Harmony)

Simple Spells for Success (Harmony)

Simple Spells for Hearth and Home (Harmony)

Marianne Williamson

Marianne has been a spiritual "mentor" of mine since the mid-eighties when her inspirational tapes on a Course in Miracles fed my soul like manna from Heaven. I love all her books but particularly her exquisite prayers and her latest exploration of romantic love as a spiritual path. You will, too.

Illuminata: A Return to Prayer (Riverhead)

Enchanted Love: The Mystical Power of Intimate Relationships (Simon & Schuster)

Joan Borysenko

Joan Borysenko has always been my spiritual trailblazer. I think of her as my personal scout, just a little bit ahead of me on my own winding and stumbling path to Wholeness. For some readers her latest book clears away the brush of confusion about what embracing spirituality from a feminine perspective really means.

A Woman's Journey to God: Finding the Feminine Path (Riverhead) A beautiful and brave book that lovingly, compassionately, and courageously embraces the truth that a woman will always begin the search for God in her heart.

Thomas Moore

Care of the Soul: A Guide for Cultivating Depth and Sacredness in Everyday Life (Harper Perennial Library) Why creating personal, daily rituals nurtures our soul and opens up our awareness of the sacred in the ordinary.

The Re-Enchantment of Everyday Life (HarperCollins) Explains why searching for wonder in our daily round is not childish but rather vital for one's existence and happiness.

The Soul of Sex (HarperCollins) Celebrates the spirituality of sex, usually ignored by psychologists and therapists, and encourages our contemplation of sex as a spiritual imperative. A brave and important book.

Julia Cameron (with Mark Bryan)

The Artist's Way: A Spiritual Path to Higher Creativity (Tarcher/Putnam) A wonderful guide to rediscovering and reclaiming your creativity. Before my own books were published, I recommended this seminal book wholeheartedly and still do. If I haven't convinced you that you're an artist of the everyday, Julia Cameron will.

Kathleen Norris

Amazing Grace: A Vocabulary of Faith (Putnam) Rethinks the intimidating language of the Christian faith and reinvents it as a welcoming source of comfort and grace.

Annie Dillard

The Writing Life (HarperCollins) Describes the challenges, tortures, joys, and passions experienced by writers on a daily basis with wry insights through personal narrative.

Anne Lamott

Bird by Bird: Some Instructions on Writing and Life (Anchor) A humorous guide to being a successful writer, filled with pithy wisdom for living with and loving your creations whether they are published or not.

Dorothy Parker

The Portable Dorothy Parker (Viking) The essential collection of witty and insightful short stories, poems, and articles from this irreverent and incomparable American writer.

Kennedy Fraser

Ornament and Silences: Essays on Women's Lives (Vintage) Fascinating reflections on women and how they behave in friendships, families, and marriages.

Patricia Lynn Reilly

A God Who Looks Like Me: Discovering a Woman-Affirming Spirituality (Ballantine) How the women in the Bible can help us find the feminine side of God and a comfortable, consoling spirituality.

Alice C. Domar, Ph.D., and Henry Dreher

Self-Nurture: Learning to Care for Yourself As Effectively As You Care for Everyone Else (Viking) A thorough and easy-to-use year-long guide that will help you transform self-nurturance from an interesting concept to a part of every woman's to-do list, written by the head of Harvard Medical School's Women's Center for Mind/Body.

Louise De Salvo

Writing As a Way of Healing (Harper San Francisco) Louise's courageous passion for binding the soul's wounds through the mystical alchemy of words and paper always moves me deeply. Both challenging and comforting, this book is an exquisite gift of grace. It can help you write yourself out of the wilderness of pain and denial into Wholeness.

Finally, a favorite form of meditation is memorizing a stanza of poetry and then letting the words wash over me. My two invariable sources of inspiration:

Collected Poems of Edna St. Vincent Millay (HarperCollins) A treasure trove of lyrical sentiments from the first woman to receive a Pulitzer Prize for poetry. In the forties she wrote, ". . . this age endowed with power / To wake the moon with footsteps. . . ."

Collected Poems of W. B. Yeats (Scribner) This collection of poems by the great Irish poet never fails, especially when my own words do.

Selected Bibliography

Ackerman, Diane. *Deep Play.* New York: Random House, 1999.

Alcott, Louisa May. *Little Women.* New York: Random House Value Publishing, 1998.

Angelou, Maya. *And I Still Rise.* New York: Random House, 1996.

Ban Breathnach, Sarah. *Simple Abundance: A Daybook of Comfort and Joy.* New York: Warner, 1995.

———*The Simple Abundance Journal of Gratitude.* New York: Warner, 1997.

———*Something More: Excavating Your Authentic Self.* New York: Warner, 1998.

———*The Illustrated Discovery Journal: Creating a Visual Autobiography of Your Authentic Self.* New York: Warner, 1999.

Borysenko, Joan. *A Woman's Journey to God: Finding the Feminine Path.* New York: Riverhead, 2000.

Branden, Nathaniel. *The Psychology of Self-Esteem: How Our Judgments about Ourselves Affect Our Success in Love and Human Relationships.* San Francisco: Jossey-Bass, 1999.

Cameron, Julia, and Mark Bryan. *The Artist's Way: A Spiritual Path to Higher Creativity.* New York: Tarcher/Putnam, 1992.

Cash, Thomas F. *What Do You See When You Look in the Mirror?: The New Body-Image Therapy for Women and Men.* New York: Bantam, 1995.

Cooper-Mullin, Alison, and Jennifer M. Coye, eds. *Once Upon a Heroine: 400 Books for Girls to Love.* Lincolnwood, Ill.: NTC Contemporary Publishing, 1998.

Selected Bibliography

Dolnick, Barrie. *Simple Spells for Love: Ancient practices for emotional fulfillment.* New York: Harmony, 1994.

———*Simple Spells for Success: Ancient practices for creating abundance and prosperity.* New York: Harmony, 1996.

———*Simple Spells for Hearth and Home: Ancient practices for creating harmony, peace and abundance.* New York: Harmony, 2000.

Dominguez, Joe, and Vicki Robin. *Your Money or Your Life: Transforming Your Relationship with Money and Achieving Financial Independence.* New York: Viking Penguin, 1993.

Glasgow, Ellen A. *The Woman Within,* Charlottesville, Va.: University Press of Virginia, 1994.

Godden, Rumer. *A House with Four Rooms.* West Seneca, N.Y.: Ulverscoft Large Print Books Limited, 1991.

Hellenga, Robert. *The Fall of a Sparrow: A Novel.* New York: Simon & Schuster, 1998.

Hillman, Carolynn. *Love Your Looks: How to Stop Criticizing and Start Appreciating Your Appearance.* New York: Simon & Schuster, 1996.

Kempe, Margery B. *Book of Margery Kempe.* New York: Viking Penguin, 1986.

Kornfield, Jack. *A Path with Heart: A Guide through the Perils and Promises of Spiritual Life.* New York: Bantam, 1993.

L'Engle, Madeleine. *The Irrational Season.* San Francisco: Harper San Francisco, 1984.

Lovric, Michelle. *How to Write Love Letters.* Knoxville, Tenn.: Shooting Star Press, 1996.

———*Love Letters: An Anthology of Passion.* Knoxville, Tenn.: Shooting Star Press, 1995.

Murdock, Maureen. *The Heroine's Journey.* Boston: Shambhala, 1998.

Needleman, Jacob. *Money and the Meaning of Life.* New York: Doubleday, 1994.

Norris, Kathleen. *Amazing Grace: A Vocabulary of Faith.* New York: Putnam, 1998.

O'Donohue, John. *Anam Cara: A Book of Celtic Wisdom.* New York: HarperCollins, 1997.

Roman, Sanaya, and Duane Packer. *Creating Money: Keys to Abundance.* Tiburon, Calif.: H.J. Kramer, Inc., 1988.

SARK (Susan Ariel Rainbow Kennedy). *A Creative Companion: How to Free Your Creative Spirit.* Berkeley, Calif.: Celestial Arts, 1995.

Scarf, Maggie. *Intimate Partners: Patterns of Love and Marriage.* New York: Ballantine, 1988.

Styron, William. *Darkness Visible: A Memoir of Madness.* New York: Random House, 1990.

van Amringe, Judyth. *Home Art: Creating Romance and Magic with Everyday Objects.* Boston: Bulfinch Press/Little, Brown, 1994.

Williams, Margery. *The Velveteen Rabbit, or How Toys Become Real.* New York: Hyperion, 1998.

Williamson, Marianne. *A Return to Love: Reflections on the Principles of a Course in Miracles.* New York: HarperCollins, 1996.

———*Illuminata: A Return to Prayer.* New York: Riverhead, 1995.

———*Enchanted Love: The Mystical Power of Intimate Relationships.* New York: Simon & Schuster, 1999.

With Thanks and Appreciation

She is a friend of my mind. She gather me, man.
The pieces I am, she gather them and give them
back to me in all the right order.

TONI MORRISON,
BELOVED

I was blessed to have my own private circle of smart, savvy, soulful and generous gatherers assist me in transforming virtually "live performance art" to the page, and I'd like to thank them all for their enormous support and authentic gifts: Sally Arteseros, Dona Cooper, Maureen Crean, Jane Wyatt Dickerson, Katie Maresca, and Ann Napolitano.

Dawne Winter, Jennifer Page, Karen Woodard, Ana Andrade, and Joslyn King perform miracles for me every day. The name of my editor at Warner Books, Caryn Karmatz Rudy, appears regularly on my gratitude list both personally and professionally. Thanks, ladies. Take a bow.

An enormous embrace to Chris Tomasino for everything. And thanks to our beloved daughters, Katie Sharp and Nora Vose, for the gift of their understanding in Italy—when both mommies unexpectedly had to work instead of play during our "vacation." Your beautiful faces at the end of each day, at home or away, are powerful reminders of what authentic success truly means.

And Oprah, of course—for holding my hand while the dream came true.

I only pray that the love and gratitude I carry in my heart for all of you can be read between the lines.